KRAIT:
THE FISHING BOAT THAT WENT TO WAR

By LYNETTE RAMSAY SILVER
WITH RESEARCH FROM MAJOR TOM HALL

*For Alison Todd,
in memory of Bill,
another Master Mariner hero,
Lynette Ramsay Silver
10.3.94*

SALLY MILNER PUBLISHING

First published in 1992 by
Sally Milner Publishing Pty Ltd
67 Glassop Street
Birchgrove NSW 2041 Australia

Reprinted in 1992

© Lynette Ramsay Silver & Major Tom Hall

Production by Sylvana Scannapiego,
Island Graphics
Design by Gatya Kelly, Doric Order
Typeset in Australia by Asset Typesetting Pty Ltd
Printed in Australia by Impact Printing, Melbourne

National Library of Australia
Cataloguing-in-Publication data:

Silver, Lynette Ramsay.
    Krait, the fishing boat that went to war.

    Bibliography.
    Includes index.
    ISBN 1 86351 063 X.

    1. Krait (Ship). 2. Operation Jaywick. 3. World War, 1939-1945
    – Naval operations, Australian. 4. World War, 1939-1945 –
    Campaigns – Singapore. I. Hall, Tom, Major. II. Title.

940.545994

All rights reserved. No part of this publication may be
reproduced, stored in a retrieval system or transmitted in
any form or by any means, electronic, mechanical,
photocopying, recording or otherwise, without prior
written permission of the copyright owners and publishers.

Distributed in Australia by Transworld Publishers

Front Cover: Tony Onorato.

Dedication

For Bill Reynolds

Acknowledgements

We gratefully acknowledge the trustees of the Australian War Memorial and the P&O Company for permission to reproduce photographic material; the assistance of all the families of the Jaywick men and also the following, many of whom supplied information and photographs from their private collections: Moss Berryman, Bert Bevan-Davies, Geoffrey Brooke, Muriel and Andrew Buie, the late K. P. Cain, Professor S. W. Carey, Rae Chambers, Les Clarke, the Albert Coates Family, Bill Cockbill, Sylvia Crane, Colonel Alan Davidson, June Davidson, Cedric Emanuel, Ross Gillett, John Grimwade, Anne Howard, Biddy and Gordon Kurtz, Lord Langford, Mary Lennox, Clive Lyon, Brenda Macduff, John MacKay, Marjorie de Malmanche, Doris Mitchell, Major Francis Moir-Byres, Major Ron Morris, Andy Munns, Mollie O'Dwyer, Brian Ogle, Tony Onorato, Roma Page, Bettina Reid, Margaret Reynolds, Don Russell, *The Northern Star* newspaper, Maggie and Chris Scott, Jack Sweeney, Arthur Suters, Marlene von Bornemann, Commander N. O. Vidgen, Kelvin Wright and Horrie Young; Kenji Akahoshi, the Fugisawa Family, Senkichi Hamagami, the Nippon Kaiji Kyokai Company, Yoshio Schimizu and Shichiro Kubo for their research in Japan; Yoshi Tosa for writing and translating all Japanese correspondence; Mick von Bornemann for translating Dutch-Indonesian documents; the Australian National Maritime Museum for its support and assistance, particularly Neil Brough, Patricia Miles and Steven Segerstrom; Amanda Turner of P&O; Deutz Australia, L. Gardner and Sons, Hawker Siddley and Ruston Diesel for supplying archival records; Ursula Davidson, Ron Gilchrist, Liz Nathan and

Acknowledgements

Moira Smythe for particular assistance with research material; the many who gave their support and assistance to Tom Hall during his research, especially Major Mike Askey, Colonel George Cardy, Joy and Norm Craig, the late Tony Wykeham-Fiennes, Alf Henricksen, Jim Sloggett, Fred Spring and Bruce Stracey. We are also especially grateful to artist Tony Onorato, Commanding Officer RVCP and of *Krait* 1977-85, whose painting of *Krait* at Pompong Island, 1943, appears on the cover of this book, and to our immediate family and friends, particularly Marie Hall and Neil Silver, for their continuing support and encouragement.

Contents

Acknowledgements iv
List of Maps   viii
Glossary of Malay Terms   ix
Krait's Specifications   x

Chapter One	**The Last Bastion**	1
Chapter Two	**Exodus**	14
Chapter Three	**Black Friday**	23
Chapter Four	**The Amazing Voyage of the** *Suey Sin Fah*	35
Chapter Five	**A Plan Unfolds**	51
Chapter Six	**Into Enemy Waters**	66
Chapter Seven	**What Price Glory?**	84
Chapter Eight	**Becalmed in Darwin**	99
Chapter Nine	**A Decline in Fortune**	115
Chapter Ten	**A Forgotten Hero**	123
Chapter Eleven	**A Revival of Fortune**	131
Chapter Twelve	**Troubled Waters**	141
Appendix I	The Capture of *Kofuku Maru*: A Case of Mistaken Identity	154
Appendix II	The Tale of Sister Edith Stevenson: Survivor	159
Appendix III	*Krait* Crew Lists	164
References	Books	167
	Despatches	
	Documents	
	Minutes, Reports, Proceedings and Newsletters	
	Newspapers, Periodicals, etc.	
	Television Documentaries	
	Private Papers	167
Index		177

Maps

Map I	The Escape Route from Singapore to the Indragiri River.
Map II	Reynolds's escape route from the Indragiri River.
Map III	Routes taken by *Krait* to and from Singapore for Operation Jaywick.
Map IV	Route taken by *Krait*, 18 September–1 October 1943, while the raiding party was away.
Map V	Routes for Operation Jaywick, Pompong I to Singapore.
Map VI	The Attack Courses for Operation Jaywick.
Map VII	*Krait*'s area of operation, 1944–1964.

Glossary of Malay Terms

kampong   a village

kolek   a small two-three man boat for fishing in sheltered waters

pagar   a large fish-trap on stilts

prahu   an ocean-going sailing vessel

pulau   an island

tandjung   a cape (geographical feature)

tonkan   any wooden boat or ship

Krait's Specifications

Built	1934, Nagahama, Japan
Construction	Teak wood
Length	21.3 metres (70′8″)
Breadth	3.6 metres (12′)
Draught	1.5 metres (5′) for'ard, 2.3 metres (7′6″) aft
Gross tonnage	68 tonnes
Original engine (1934)	Deutz PMV 230 model. 4 cylinder, 2 stroke diesel. 430 RPM, 100 HP. Maximum speed 8½ knots. Engine number 171583-586. One of 188 engines manufactured by Deutz, Koln, Germany, between 1927-30.
Replacement engine (1943)	Gardner 6L3 model. 6 cylinder diesel. 650 RPM, 110 HP. Maximum speed 6½ knots. Engine number 54512. Range 8000 miles. Manufactured by L. Gardner and Sons, England.

CHAPTER ONE

The Last Bastion

The tall, rangy Australian stood upon the wharf at Singapore's Telok Ayer Basin seemingly oblivious of the panic raging round him. Beyond the dockside, the waters of Keppel Harbour heaved with a confused tangle of twisted and splintered wreckage, while high above, the sun was shrouded by smoke from huge oil fires that filled the air with the acrid smell of burning fuel. Away from the wharf majestic colonial buildings, many of them still amazingly unscathed, looked down upon streets crammed with frightened and scurrying civilians. Despite their frenetic activity, the people were making little headway. The Australian seethed with barely suppressed anger at the sight. Smugly confident that the might of the British Empire would overcome all threats to their security, the citizens of Singapore had made their move far too late. Indeed, he reflected, it had not been until the Japanese were at the city's gates that the appalling truth had been rammed home — Singapore, the impregnable fortress, must soon fall.

This state of affairs, brought about by the failure of local and British authorities to face reality, came as no surprise to the Australian. Having come under enemy attack weeks before, Captain William Roy Reynolds, Master Mariner, had no illusions about the Japanese. Like all those up-country who had not been warned of the imminent danger of invasion, he had been caught unawares when the Japanese had attacked northern Malaya on 8 December 1941, barely three months previously. But, unlike the majority, Reynolds had not fled. While the Europeans had beaten a retreat to the supposed safety of Singapore and the

Malays had sought refuge in limestone caves, he had reported for duty with the Local Defence Corps at Ipoh, the provincial town in Perak state where he was employed by the Anglo-Oriental Mining Company.

His job of organising the compulsory evacuation of civilians after the first bombs fell on Ipoh on December 15 had been a nightmare. As if the terror created by the air raid was not enough, various officials, without any reference to each other, had issued a series of conflicting orders which had turned an orderly evacuation into absolute chaos. On December 23, after a direct hit on a laden ammunition train had set nearby oil storage tanks ablaze, the handful of Europeans still in the area were ordered to move south. Reynolds refused to budge. Although his status was strictly that of a volunteer civilian, there was no way known that this forty-nine-year-old mining engineer was going to leave vital supplies and facilities intact for the rapidly approaching enemy.

As the Japanese, mounted on bicycles, had ridden by the thousands down the well-sealed roads of Malaya, their advance barely checked by inexperienced Indian troops who had been set the impossible task of holding the northern frontier, Reynolds had swung into action. An expert in the art of demolition from years of mining experience, Reynolds, with a swag of dynamite slung under one arm, had aligned himself with a group of army engineers in the northern command zone. As the Japanese swarmed down the Malay peninsula, Reynolds and members of 3rd Field Company, Bombay Sappers and Miners, had kept one step ahead, blowing up in quick succession telegraph stations, power stations, telephone exchanges and installations such as the tin mining plant belonging to Reynolds's employer at Malim Nawar, just south of Ipoh. With tin in short supply, the destruction of this plant was of enormous importance, particularly since orders from the Malayan military to demolish Penang's Eastern Tin Smelting Works and its 4000 tonnes of tin had been received far too late, providing resource-starved Japan with a priceless windfall.

When Reynolds finally arrived in Singapore on January 19, he had been in action long enough to be under no illusion as to the so-called invincibility of the island. In spite of fierce fighting by members of the Australian Eighth Division and a battalion of Argyll and Sutherland Highlanders — the only jungle-trained troops to hand — it was obvious that Japanese domination of Malaya was all but complete. Eleven days later, when thousands of civilian refugees, followed by the tattered remnants of the British army, had streamed across the causeway that linked Singapore with Malaya, Reynolds's worst fears were confirmed. Unless a miracle occurred, Singapore was destined to become another Dunkirk.

Unlike the situation at the French channel port, where the British Army had been successfully evacuated by thousands of naval and volunteer civilian craft, Reynolds knew that Singapore could hold out no hope of rescue from the outside. If the million or so civilians and troops crammed onto the island were to be evacuated to safety, it would have to be organised from within.

With this in mind, Reynolds, on his arrival in Singapore city, had reported as instructed to the Chief Man Power Officer, Mr R. J. Farrer, who sent him off to several potential jobs. To Reynolds's chagrin, nobody wanted him, least of all the officials stationed on HMS *Laburnum*, an engineless hulk that had been converted into naval offices. Among the sundry naval staff housed on the former WWI Flower Class sloop were the Naval Shipping Transport Officer, who was organising evacuations, and Captain Mulock, a former Royal Naval officer who had been brought out of retirement to take charge of all auxiliary vessels. Wishing to do something constructive, Reynolds had gone to *Laburnum* to seek permission to put into working order a motley and rapidly deteriorating collection of Japanese fishing boats, which he had noticed previously, tied up beside the wharf at Telok Ayer.

Had Reynolds had any previous dealings with the military administration he would not have bothered to waste his time putting forward such a proposition. The Navy was not interested and, before sending him packing, informed Reynolds that the dilapidated craft were beyond salvation, thereby demonstrating that it, too, was a victim of the same short-sightedness that had afflicted Singapore's officialdom for months, if not years.

Indeed, such was the lassitude in the upper echelons of the British Army that, even when invasion became almost certain, Lieutenant-General Arthur Percival, Singapore's senior officer, had refused to listen to reason. Despite impassioned pleas to do something, quickly, every recommendation by Chief Engineer Ivan Simson to build defence works had fallen on deaf ears, as had requests to organise a civil defence unit.

Appeals to the Governor had been just as futile. Sir Shenton Thomas, unwilling and unable to face reality, had clung and continued to cling to his belief that Singapore would stand, despite every indication to the contrary. Ostrich-like, he had ignored orders from England to evacuate all 'useless mouths', sending back empty to their home ports ships which had ferried men and materials to Singapore. Consequently, on 8 February 1942, the day on which the Japanese began their final onslaught across the narrow Straits of Johore, a horrified Reynolds observed that Singapore, far from being a fortified citadel, was overflowing with defenceless women and children.

With the civic and military leaders pretending for weeks that all was well, it had taken the unexpectedly aggressive actions of the Japanese, combined with tales of terror brought by refugees flooding into the city, to finally prod the citizens into action. Not even the initial bombing of Singapore in the early hours of December 8, timed to coincide with the invasion of Malaya, had been taken very seriously — particularly when there were no more raids on the city itself for another three weeks. Although air raids had increased markedly in January, most European civilians had considered war to be a situation more exciting than alarming, marvelling at the aerial dog-fights and swarming in great numbers to gawk at the damage inflicted by the enemy bombers.

Perhaps it was just as well that the civilians were kept in the dark. Apart from some air-raid shelters constructed in the gardens of rich Europeans (more as a talking point than anything else), nothing had been organised in the way of shelter. The casualties that had occurred had not created undue alarm among the British, since they had been confined largely to the locals. As Japanese bombs had rained down, the flimsy houses of Chinatown, unlike the sturdily built British bungalows, had simply collapsed like packs of cards, burying alive or killing outright thousands of people whose bodies were never recovered from the rubble.

Yet, in spite of the growing numbers of casualties during January the civilians, European and Singaporean alike, had made

The Last Bastion

virtually no attempt to flee. Constantly reassured by military leaders and senior administrators (Sir Shenton Thomas in particular) that all was well, they had kept up the pretence that a state of emergency did not exist.

By late January, the Navy alone had changed its tune. Only nine days after Reynolds's visit to *Laburnum*, the Senior Service had been jolted — if not to action stations then at least to action — by a heavy bombing attack on its magnificent and recently completed Naval Base. Naval staff, like all Air Force personnel who were not needed, had left in such haste that almost the entire base — supplies, equipment and facilities — had been left intact. When Bill Reynolds had turned up a few days later to assist with a spot of demolition, ordered in a belated attempt to prevent the world's most up-to-date base falling into Japanese hands, the alacrity with which the naval personnel had quit their posts was plainly evident in the plates piled with food and half-empty tea cups left sitting upon hurriedly vacated mess tables.

This abrupt evacuation, coming hard on the heels of the Navy's snooty rejection of Reynolds, might have led to his deciding to call it quits had not his morale, and the morale of many, received an unexpected boost by the defiant attitude of a lowly ranked British soldier a few days later.

On January 30, with the Japanese in hot pursuit and Malaya a shambles, the British army had begun its retreat across the Straits of Johore to Singapore. As the 30 000 battle-weary troops trudged to safety with a straggling crocodile of refugees, the engineers waited anxiously, hoping to delay the Japanese advance by blowing a hole in the causeway that linked the most southerly tip of the Malay peninsula with Singapore Island.

At the end of the column was the rearguard and, dawdling along at the very tail of the rearguard, was Drummer Hardy, an Argyll and Sutherland Highlander. When the Argyll's commanding officer Colonel Stewart saw that Hardy, a man who had never been known to run, was taking his time, he exhorted him to get a move on. However, the Colonel's psychological pep-talks that the Japanese were nothing special had been heeded well by the bandsman. As he had not run from the enemy to date, Hardy could see no reason why he should do so now. Despite his CO's entreaties to step on it, Hardy continued to maintain his careful measured walk.

As the new day dawned, with the defenders of Singapore watching his every agonising step and the demolition experts itching to push their plungers, Drummer Hardy, now alone on the causeway, finally crossed the Straits of Johore. In so doing, he earned for himself an undying place in history, not only as the last man to leave Malaya but also as a most unlikely hero, who dismissed protests over his lack of haste with a laconic 'Japs are only Japs and it is undignified for an Argyll to take any notice of them'.

Whilst undeniably the stuff of which legends are made, Hardy's disdain for the Japanese was not unique. Indeed, such was the feeling of British invincibility that many citizens believed the retreat from Malaya had been nothing more than a ploy to lure the Japanese into Singapore so that the British could fight them on their own patch — a misconception that was strengthened by the Governor suggesting, even as the troops withdrew across the causeway, that citizens with green thumbs should start planting vegetables in case supplies from the traditional Chinese market gardens dried up. He added that anyone moved to do so would be supplied with fertiliser free of charge. Consequently, it was not until Japan's 'softening up' of the island on February 8, when the enemy barrage filled the air with the thunderous roar of heavy artillery, that long held views on Singapore's security were really shattered.

One of those who decided the time had come to leave was the senior Malayan RNVR officer, Commander Bailey, who had inherited the important post of Captain Auxiliary Vessels from Captain Mulock on February 1. Although he had tried to ensure his safety by moving from *Laburnum* to an office block in town, he now concluded that Singapore was no place to be and, despite direct orders from his Admiral to return to his post, sailed for Java on February 10.

Although orders were issued for his arrest, the threat of retribution from even one as exalted as an Admiral was evidently no deterrent to others. Within two days all harbour officials had also left and the Shipping Transport Officer was busily preparing to follow suit. Within hours of Commander Bailey's unauthorised

The Last Bastion

departure Reynolds, realising that the situation was about to become very sticky, returned to the wharf at Telok Ayer. Still sitting there, unwanted and unloved, were the Japanese fishing boats which had been simply left to their fate.

Part of an original fleet of forty-five, they had been prevented from leaving town on the outbreak of war not by the Navy but by Mr A. H. 'Dickie' Dickinson, the Inspector-General of Police, who wore several hats. Besides being the chief law-enforcer, he also controlled the Local Defence Forces to which Reynolds belonged and had, since 1939, kept tabs on all aliens, particularly the Japanese. Following a well orchestrated plan, since most of Malaya's 7900 Japanese immigrants were believed, one way or another, to work for Japanese intelligence, Dickie Dickinson had moved with lightning rapidity on the morning of December 8 to ensure that no fishing vessels left port and that the 1200 Japanese whom he knew to be in town were rounded up.

As the Navy had scathingly pointed out to Reynolds, most of the vessels Dickinson had swooped upon were incapable of going anywhere. Some had vital engine parts missing while others were so unseaworthy they would not have made it past the inner harbour. Casting his expert eye over what was left of the fleet, by now looking even more weatherworn and dilapidated than ever, Reynolds began to formulate a plan. Provided he could kick one of the ramshackle tubs into life, he too might be able to skedaddle before the Japanese arrived.

Although Reynolds was no longer a young man, such a plan was definitely not beyond his capabilities. Not only was the Australian a skilled engineer and sailor, he had also spent the best part of twenty years in Burma, Malaya and the islands of the East Indies. Born in 1892, within sight and smell of the sea at Brighton on Melbourne's Port Phillip Bay, he had spent his boyhood in the busy, bustling port of Williamstown. The inopportune death of his father in a rail accident had taken Bill, still not much more than a lad, out of the classroom and into the merchant marine. Highly intelligent and a brilliant mathematician, he had risen steadily in seniority, obtaining his Master's Ticket at Dundee, Scotland in 1918. By this time, with the British Empire embroiled in the Great War, he had been recruited into the Royal Naval Reserve, serving as a Sub-Lieutenant and then

Caricature of Bill Reynolds, aged 50, by original Jaywick member, Don Russell.

Lieutenant in several ships of the Dover Patrol before being given command of *Firmament*, one of four small merchant vessels which had been taken into naval service for minesweeping and antisubmarine duties. As hostilities were over by this time, *Firmament* had assisted in salvage and harbour reconstruction duties in Zeebrugge, a Belgian port used by the Germans as a submarine base until it had been blocked by a British naval raid in April 1918.

Seven months after the Armistice, Reynolds was demobbed. However, before returning to Australia to rejoin the Merchant Marine, he took the plunge into matrimony, marrying his Scottish-born sweetheart, Bridget (Bessie) O'Brien, in Dover on Boxing Day 1919.

During the next few years, operating mainly out of Hong Kong, Captain Reynolds sailed the oceans of the world, carrying mixed cargoes from one exotic port to another and often ferrying Muslim pilgrims to and from the Arabian city of Jidda, from where they made the overland journey from the Red Sea to the holy Islamic city of Mecca. While his passengers were busy ashore, Reynolds continued on his journey, delivering and picking up cargo from ports such as Genoa and Barcelona, before collecting his pilgrims and returning to the Far East.

By the end of 1925, following a run of very bad luck, he had had enough. His troubles had begun on 29 July 1923 when, due to the incompetence of the vessel's third engineer, a fire had started in the engine room of his ship, SS *Ferrara*, of which he had just taken charge. Despite Reynolds's best efforts, the fire spread and the ship had to be abandoned off the island of Sabang, Northern Sumatra.

Eight months later he lost his second ship, when SS *Frangestan*, laden with a cargo of cotton and linseed and with 1221 pilgrims and fifteen European passengers on board, caught fire in the Red Sea while en route to Jidda. Although Reynolds had been exonerated of all blame and, indeed, commended for evacuating everyone, including his crew of thirty-nine unscathed, and for his innovative techniques in trying to save the ship by piping carbon dioxide (which he was carrying as part of his cargo) into the burning hold to try and quell the fire, he was fed up. With both ships a total loss, the investigations had taken weeks, and, although he had emerged with his reputation not only intact but enhanced, he decided it was time to call it quits. Realising also that his prolonged absences were not conducive to harmonious family living Reynolds, evidently with few qualms, resigned command of his next vessel, SS *Setstan*, in September 1925.

In a complete turn around, he accepted a position as a dredgemaster with Thompsons, a Victorian foundry firm with mining interests in Borneo and with whom he had family connections. Four years later, his idyllic and profitable existence in the tropics was temporarily interrupted when his employer became one of the many casualties of the Depression. But Reynolds was not idle for long. Snapped up almost immediately by Theodore and Company, another Australian mining corporation, he managed the Taungpila Mine at Tavoy in Lower Burma before accepting a similar post with Anglo-Oriental at the tin-smelting works at Ipoh.

Until the Japanese had put paid to everything, Reynolds, a congenial host, bon vivant and great raconteur, had revelled in an oppulent and refined way of life that was in sharp contrast to the rough-and-tough image he projected to his sea-going fraternity. At first glance this lanky, almost gauntly lean man, whose weatherbeaten features added at least ten years to his age, appeared an unlikely contender to make a dash across enemy controlled waters. However, looks were deceptive. The chameleon-like Reynolds, with his vast and varied experience and his ability to converse fluently in Malay, was better equipped than most to undertake such a task.

Reynolds's decision on February 10 to quit Singapore had come none too soon. For the past two days, ever since the Japanese had poured across the Straits of Johore from Malaya, the Allies had been retreating in an ever decreasing circle. When General Archibald Wavell, Commander-in-Chief of American, British, Dutch and Australian Forces, had arrived that very morning from his headquarters in Java to assess the situation, he ordered the RAF to plough up the airfields, destroy all ammunition and fuel supplies and leave at once for the Dutch East Indies. Wavell, who informed British Prime Minister Winston Churchill that the 'battle was not going well', would leave Singapore the next day 'without much confidence of any prolonged resistance'.

If Wavell, not to mention Commander Bailey, had received the message loud and clear, so too, Reynolds observed, had many civilians. With the constant barrage of artillery, the almost uninterrupted air-raids, the nauseating stench from decomposing corpses and the terrifying sound of gunfire clearly audible, they were now attempting to leave Singapore in droves.

The panic, which had begun shortly after the barrage began, was now frantic. Chinese and Malays, who had no hope of evacuation, ran in every direction, mingling with deserters who were looking for booty before they fled the area. There was wholesale looting in every quarter of the city, with normally law-abiding housewives scampering about bombed warehouses and stores, loaded with foodstuffs and anything else that they thought might come in handy. Behind Telok Ayer, city streets pocked with shell holes were strewn with overturned trams and motor vehicles. All roads still open into the city were rapidly becoming impassable, choked with cars and military trucks, whose way had been blocked by abandoned vehicles, engines still running as their owners sought refuge from bombing attacks. Fires cast crazy lights across shells of buildings, some of which tottered alarmingly before crashing to the ground in clouds of dusty masonry, filling alley ways and monsoon drains with rubble. Overhead, severed electricity cables dangled from snapped and broken poles, showering the area with blue sparks as the live wires danced an erratic and deadly jig.

At Clifford Pier, a short distance along the quayside from where Reynolds stood, the scene was absolute chaos as hundreds battled to secure a place on board a ship. All those trying to board without tickets or officially issued passes were sent back down the crowded gangplanks, jostling with those who were clawing their way up. Quite oblivious to the bedlam taking place on the waterfront, the P&O shipping line was still selling tickets, with the cool-headed staff simply transferring their business nine kilometres inshore to the manager's private residence when the town office was bombed. Here prospective passengers, who had previously shunned tickets to 'unsuitable' places such as Australia and India, formed long queues along the tree-lined driveway, desperate for anything that was offered, provided it was as far away from Singapore as possible.

To their consternation, loyal Malay and Chinese maritime staff found their jobs on merchant ships reallocated to Europeans, many of whom were completely unqualified to hold the positions. Although special travel passes were issued to selected civil servants and families of defence personnel, none were available to non-British subjects, which meant in effect that Chinese, Malays and Indians did not rate at all. Eurasian civilians, whose part-British parentage or marriage to Europeans gave them the required status, were rejected if they could not provide official documentation. Those unable, because of losses sustained by bombing or fire, to produce sufficient evidence to satisfy the form-loving bureaucrats were left behind while others sailed to safety.

As the frenzied activity along the dockside continued unabated, orders were issued to implement a scorched earth policy and destroy anything that might be of use to the enemy. When the large oil storage tank at Bukit Timah was set alight, black smoke from the spectacular blaze billowed into the sky for three days, blotting out the sunlight and returning to the earth as oily sludge every time it rained. The burning of the oil was followed by the destruction of other fuel reserves, supplies, ammunition, guns and equipment. The sight of bank officials feeding huge bonfires with treasury notes was just as startling as that of monsoon drains awash with thousands of litres of liquor dumped from cellars and bond stores.

It was against this backdrop of unremitting noise and devastation that Reynolds analysed his situation. In light of the present desperate circumstances, the rounding up of a crew willing to help him sail to freedom did not appear to be a problem, although supplies, fuel, weapons and ammunition might be a little more tricky. The most difficult part would be to find an ocean-going vessel seaworthy enough to make a dash across enemy-patrolled waters and inconspicuous enough to avoid attracting the attention of Japanese aircraft. With all other suitable craft privately owned or already earmarked, Reynolds's choice was narrowed down to the moth-eaten Japanese fishing fleet, long since abandoned. Since orders had been given to scuttle or burn all vessels not required for evacuation purposes, he knew it was a case of now or never.

Any problem that may have arisen over Reynolds's decision to salvage one of these vessels before they either went up in smoke or were sunk at their moorings was solved when he was 'given' one by Dickinson, either directly or through his deputy Mr F. D. Bisseker, a mining colleague of Reynolds who, after a great deal of bullying, had finally forced the authorities to organise a civil defence unit. Such was Bisseker's energy that he was now not only Deputy Director of Civil Defence but also Director of Labour and Transport. Unlike the naval officials, these stalwart civilians were still at their posts and it seems that they had inherited by default the responsibility for all transportation. With permission granted, and with no one left in authority on the now almost deserted *Laburnum* to kick up a fuss or tell him otherwise, Reynolds, after a quick appraisal, finally settled on a ship that looked a little less disreputable than the rest. With a brief 'She'll do' to no one in particular, Reynolds was in business.

His choice could hardly have been described as inspiring. She was a small, nondescript, narrow-gutted vessel, not much more than a motorised sampan. From the noisome odour wafting from her holds and permeating every timber, it was not difficult for Reynolds to deduce in which area of maritime activity she had been previously employed. She was a Japanese fishing boat, registered number 2283 and her name was *Kofuku Maru*.

CHAPTER TWO

Exodus

Reynolds was first to admit that *Kofuku Maru*, which meant 'Happiness' or 'Good Fortune', did not live up to her name. Neither did she look much of a ship. Indeed, it was obvious from the Navy's derogatory comments that her riff-raff appearance, coupled with her distinctly fishy smell, were the reasons she had not been appropriated long before this. Reynolds knew that had she appeared less derelict, it would have been a different story, for, although Japanese owned and operated, she did not look typically Asian to western eyes. Indeed, the Japanese had been so successful in adopting European design to their own needs that *Kofuku Maru*, like many Japanese fishing vessels, was very similar in construction to that of driftnet fishing boats operating out of English ports in East Anglia.

Yet at the time of her capture she was not being used in this capacity. Built in 1934 in Nagahama, Japan, a small port on the Inland Sea on the island of Shikoku, she was now a fish carrier and very typical of the vessels being made at the Hamagami shipyards, one of about five shipyards operating in Nagahama at that time. It would appear that the design on which she was based was extremely flexible, allowing ships to be adapted for driftnet fishing and fish carrying, as well as all-purpose vessels for ferrying goods and passengers.

It was a type of craft that Reynolds knew well. *Firmament*, the ship he had commanded while serving with the Royal Navy in the Great War, had been a drifter before she had been commissioned for war service. Judging by the number of similar craft that plied the waters around Singapore, it was a style as much suited to Asian fishermen and their methods, as those of the North Sea.

Constructed by artisans who passed their skills from one generation to the next and who did not work to formal plans, *Kofuku Maru* was smaller than her English counterpart, being a mere twenty-one metres in length and a scant three and a half in width. She was also more spartan, being bereft of any crew facilities, apart from a narrow bunk that also served as a seat for the helmsman, which had been squeezed into a pokey, barely two-metre-square wheelhouse. Above the bunk was a fold-down chart-table, which so restricted space when in use that the helmsman had to move to one side, making it impossible to steer the ship with any degree of accuracy. Since the table, when in the down position, was only thirty centimetres above the bunk, any member of the crew who had the misfortune to be catching up on forty winks when the charts needed to be consulted had to be unceremoniously ejected from his bed.

Situated below the two-centimetre-thick teak deck and immediately behind the wheelhouse was the engine room. In it was a Deutz four-cylinder diesel engine. The sturdy German-made machine, a 1927-30 model, was evidently the original, and Reynolds noted that it was in surprisingly good condition, having been well maintained by its previous owners. Immediately behind the long, low platform, into which six glass side panels had been set to form an elevated engine-room housing, was a small storage hatch and beyond that, the stern. Apart from the wheelhouse itself, the only other protection from the elements was that provided by a rather tatty canvas awning, which more or less covered the deck from the wheelhouse to the stern. Evidently, the repair of the awning was of low priority, since the ship had been used as a shuttle service, carrying supplies to, and fish from, the Anambas Islands fishing fleet, rather than operating as an offshore, long-term fishing boat.

Although he had been in no position to put a stop to it, Dickie Dickinson, whose job it was to monitor the activities by Japanese fishermen, had found this wandering by Japanese fishing boats to and fro across South-East Asian waters highly suspicious. Aware that Singapore was alive with Japanese agents and realising also that the alien fishing vessels could be used to guide hostile ships into British-held territory, he had closely watched the movements of all Japanese fishermen and their craft.

In *Kofuku Maru*'s case, it seems that his suspicions were well-founded. The appearance of the vessel, on a Japanese government list in 1939, indicates that espionage may have been of more importance than fish carrying. Whether or not her owners, the Fujisawa family (headed by Kotaro Fugisawa whose given name, containing the Chinese character for 'fortune', had evidently inspired the name *Kofuku Maru*), knew of any clandestine activities is not known. However, the suspicion that she may not have been what she appeared to be is strengthened by the fact that shortly before the Japanese had attacked various targets on 8 December 1941, two of *Kofuku Maru*'s sister ships, *Shofuku Maru* (Small Fortune) and *Fukufu Maru* (Fortune of Wind) — both of which had carried a 'seaman' who looked too aristocratic to be a simple fisherman — had been in areas where attacks had been launched.

Spy ship or no, Reynolds conceded that *Kofuku Maru*, with her name and number painted in regulation block letters on her bow, looked no different to any other run-of-the-mill Japanese fishing boat. There was no special equipment on board — far from it. Navigational aids, apart from a compass, were non-existent, and Reynolds knew that it would be vital to keep a sharp lookout through the three wheelhouse windows, whose frames, along with those of the two clip-back doors, had been picked out in a grubby shade of white. There was no evidence of a wireless, nor of any aerial. Indeed, the only installations of any height aft were the three pipes protruding through the canopy — two to extract exhaust from the engine and the generator motor, and the other to act as a ventilation shaft for the engine room. Further back, in the stern itself, was a bucket on a rope. Known as a 'head' in nautical circles, this most unsophisticated and unsanitary lavatory arrangement afforded no privacy whatsoever. Right alongside, without any concession to the most basic rudiments of hygiene, was a tiny galley, containing a small petrol stove and a primitive, vented oven.

For'ard of the wheelhouse, ranged in a row towards the bow were four hatches leading to four cork-lined, insulated holds, into which seventeen tonnes of fish could be crammed. Beyond the

Exodus

holds, and almost in the bow, was a single mast which, when required, could be lowered out of the way to rest in a shallow crutch — a cradle-like affair attached to the roof of the wheelhouse. There was no sign of any sail. In any case the sail for this type of vessel, being designed simply to keep the vessel square to the wind while drifting over the fishing grounds, was virtually useless as a method of propulsion. There was also no windlass and only light ground tackle. Perhaps, all things considered, the only real attribute about which *Kofuku Maru* could boast, apart from the reliable engine which was capable of a speed of eight and a half knots, was her seaworthiness. The black-painted Formosan teak hull, sheathed below the waterline with a type of copper-based material known as Muntz metal, was so solidly constructed that the forty-seven-tonne vessel could be careened, rather than docked, for repairs.

The ship had ceased to function as a Japanese fishing vessel on 8 December 1941, when she had the misfortune to be in port when war broke out. Confined to the basin at Telok Ayer on the orders of Dickie Dickinson, she had not joined her sister ships *Fukuyu Maru 2163* (Fortune of Excellence) and *Shofuku Maru 2205*, which, being out to sea, had been among those taken as prize ships by the Royal Australian Navy and impounded.

By the time Reynolds had found *Kofuku Maru*, her sister ships were no more. The navy, under orders to enforce the strict scorched earth policy, had sunk all auxilliary craft lest they fall into Japanese hands. However, such was the similarity of the three Japanese vessels in name and appearance that it was to be *Kofuku Maru* which would attain notoriety, in the mistaken belief that she had been the first Japanese ship captured by the RAN in the Pacific Zone. (See Appendix I)

Having selected the erstwhile fishing vessel, Reynolds left the wharf and disappeared into the myriad of twisting, crowded streets of nearby Chinatown. A short time later he re-emerged, followed by one Ah Tee and seven other Chinese, whom he had rounded up from a local boarding house. For the rest of that day and into the night, while the oil inferno at Bukit Timah cast an eerie glow over the docks and Churchill's latest message to fight on to the death was being digested, work on *Kofuku Maru* progressed at a fast rate. Aided by his willing team, Reynolds toiled with a vengeance, reconditioning the engine, scrounging fuel oil and generally making the ship seaworthy.

At dusk on February 11, having spent another day on the job without a break, Reynolds began combing Singapore for provisions. It was not the easiest of tasks but by ten o'clock the next morning he had managed to acquire quite a load and announced that the boat would leave immediately. Without further ado, and with no fanfare whatever, *Kofuku Maru* slipped her mooring and sailed a short distance to Blakang Mati Island, where Reynolds stopped to pick up two Englishmen, who were also Perak defence volunteers. Engineer Alec Elliott, a fifty-one-year-old who hailed from Swindon, and London-born Harold Papworth, a twenty-four-year-old who had volunteered to act as seaman, had been billetted on the island by the Straits Trading Company Works, evidently to assist with the demolition of tin smelters on nearby Pulau Brani.

Kofuku Maru was merely one ship among many to leave port that day. Although quite a flotilla was already steaming south, the number of ships departing that morning had been bolstered by the overnight dropping of twenty-nine wooden boxes each containing a letter from Percival's Japanese counterpart, General Yamashita, urging surrender. Baulking at capitulation for the present, Percival nevertheless decided to destroy as much military hardware as possible and evacuate immediately a large number of women, children, nursing sisters, technical and shore-based naval staff. In the early hours of the morning a hurriedly assembled convoy had sailed south under the protection of the cruiser *Durban* and destroyers *Stronghold* and *Jupiter*. Unfortunately, the embarkation had not passed without incident. Suspecting, quite rightly as it turned out, that this convoy might be the last to escape unscathed, a group of army deserters had forced its way on board *Empire Star*, shooting dead the dockyard captain in the process.

Towards noon, while the *Durban* convoy was threading its way through the islands towards the safety of Java, *Kofuku Maru* was heading across Singapore's outer harbour. As the ship neared the Singapore Strait, twenty-seven Japanese bombers plastered the area with high explosive. Miraculously, *Kofuku Maru* managed to avoid annihilation by scuttling into the shelter of St John's

Island, about six kilometres from Blakang Mati. While she lay there drifting, Reynolds made himself useful by shouting directions to troops trying to make a getaway to the south in sundry motorised craft.

It was just as well that Reynolds was occupied sufficiently to prevent his venturing into open water before the coast was reasonably clear. Just over 100 kilometres to the south the bombers had caught up with a small fleet of ships — two old Yangtse River gunboats, *Grasshopper* and *Dragonfly*, which were escorting two paddle-steamers and a tugboat. By the time the twenty-seven aircraft had finished unleashing their bombs, all the vessels had been either sunk or blown to bits, killing all but fifty of the 400 passengers. Unfortunately, the odds of survival closer to Singapore were no better. As Australian naval officer G. A. Keith recorded, to risk exposure, even in the harbour, was foolhardy in the extreme:

> The air-raid siren commenced wailing when I reached the T-piece jetty in the Singapore Roads. It gave scant warning of the raid. The Jap bombers were already visible, coming in from seaward as I quickly took shelter behind sandbags. Hundreds of sampans and launches were tied up between the shore and the jetty which ran parallel to it. Movement ceased everywhere. The swarming populace went to earth or into hiding. Alone in the expectant stillness, a sturdy Chinaman stood at his work, slowly rowing a sampan towards the shore with rhythmical strokes. The planes passed overhead and bombs exploded across the anchorage and among the shipping in rapid succession. As though by the wave of a magical wand, the Chinaman and his sampan were transformed into a burst of flame and brown smoke. Only a small, dark stain on the placid waters of the bay remained to mark their passing.

With Reynolds too busy to make a dash for it, it was more good luck than good judgment that such a hideous fate did not overtake *Kofuku Maru* and her crew. However, by 1.30 pm Reynolds became fed up with the waiting and ventured out of his hiding place to take a look towards Durian Strait, where most of the craft were heading. Deciding that way was fraught with danger, he changed course for the less direct, but infinitely safer and better protected route down the Riouw Strait. While other ships attempted to run the gauntlet of enemy bombers to the south, Reynolds and his crew sailed in an easterly direction, encountering no further trouble as they crossed the forty kilometres of open sea that lay between Singapore and the islands of the Riouw Archipelago. At eight that evening, when the ship finally arrived at the sprawling, ramshackle town of Tandjung Pinang situated on the south-western corner of Bintan Island, Reynolds was in for a shock. The Dutch, taking one look at what they believed to be a Japanese fishing vessel, placed the ship under arrest.

The mistake was eventually ironed out the following morning when the Dutch discovered that Reynolds was a friend and not a foe. Having just weathered an air-raid, they were even more pleased to make his acquaintance when he offered to evacuate 266 dependents of the local Indonesian garrison to Rengat, a small settlement on the uppermost navigable reaches of Sumatra's Indragiri River. By the time *Kofuku Maru* left that night Reynolds had managed to sandwich fifty refugees on board the tiny Japanese vessel and crammed the rest on board a disabled island trader named *Silver Gull*, which *Kofuku Maru* took in tow. The inauspicious date of their departure for Rengat was one which Reynolds and thousands of others would have cause to remember — Friday, February 13.

As the two ships made their slow passage from Riouw across the Berhala Strait to Sumatra, hiding by day and sailing by night, the situation in Singapore was deteriorating alarmingly — so much so that General Percival issued orders to evacuate as many people as possible by clearing the harbour of small craft. Unfortunately, while hundreds of women, children, medical staff and non-combatant military were being loaded on to a thirteen-vessel convoy, the wharves and the harbour were once again heavily bombed by the Japanese.

By this stage, it was almost impossible to maintain any semblance of order. Authorised evacuees stampeded on board the nearest vessel, some did not turn up at all, while others, taking advantage of the situation, illegally grabbed the spaces that were left. Such was the disorder that some senior civil servants, who had been ordered to remain behind, quit their posts and joined the rush. One of this group determined to leave without permission was Mr Rex Nunn, head of the Public Works Department. Claiming that as a Group Captain in the RAFVR he had vital dispatches to deliver for the Governor, he secured a place for himself and his wife and was well away before his absence was detected. Little did Mr Nunn realise that he had talked his way out of the frying pan and into the fire.

Unable to decipher a warning that was sent by the Dutch on February 10 (owing to an inexplicably premature destruction of the code books), the British had no idea that Japanese ships had been ordered to rendezvous on February 13 in the Bangka Strait, prior to an attack on Palembang. Oblivious to the terror that waited off the coast of southern Sumatra the thirteen small ships, accompanied by many others which were attempting to flee independently, voyaged south — straight into the heart of the Japanese fleet.

Later that afternoon, unaware of the appalling fate that was soon to overtake so many, Percival held a conference with his generals. Although orders had just been received from Wavell that they were to 'fight it out to the end', the commanders were unanimous that Percival should seek wider discretionary powers, believing that 'there must come a stage when in the interests of the troops and civil population further bloodshed will serve no useful purpose'.

Faced with the choice of either surrendering or mounting a counter-attack to regain control of the water supply, fuel and food dumps — an action which would inevitably result in the slaughter of the civilian population — Percival applied for, and finally received, the permission he sought. On the morning of February 15, with the blessing of both Wavell and Churchill, the British general announced to his senior officers that capitulation was the only sane course of action.

After a very one-sided parley with the Japanese at Bukit Timah, the terms of surrender dictated by the victors were accepted by the vanquished. The instructions were quite straightforward. The cease-fire would take place at 8.30 pm. The next morning, after lining the streets to witness the triumphal entry into Singapore by representatives of the Imperial Japanese Army, all Allied troops would lay down their arms and become prisoners of war.

There were thousands, however, who were unwilling to accept the inevitability of capture. With only hours in which to make good their escape they left for Sumatra, the only route now open, in anything that could float. While many high-ranking officers and civil servants made the journey in style, aboard luxury launches belonging to local sultanates, others were forced to resort to more humble forms of transport. Gunners and engineers, long considered to be among the more intellectual members of the army and who for years had studiously avoided anything remotely associated with the sea, learned by frustrating trial and error how to keep Chinese-style junks and sampans off the mudbanks and in the water. Other enterprising individuals, unable to acquire such vessels, resorted to more innovative methods. One rugged Australian army captain, on finding himself alone in his escape bid, solved his pressing transportation problem by rousing an elderly Chinese man from his bed, and forcing him at gunpoint to climb into a small dinghy and begin rowing. He ultimately rowed his passenger all the way to Sumatra, his tired muscles receiving the necessary bursts of adrenalin to do so by a few judicious waves of the officer's pistol.

Following in the wake of the scores of vessels that had already begun the perilous journey south, these daring and often desperate souls entered the Japanese-infested waters of Sumatra at about the same time that Reynolds, who had avoided the enemy by only the most slender of margins, was navigating the many channels which criss-crossed the mangrove-clustered entrance to the Indragiri River. As the *Kofuku Maru* sought sanctuary in the muddy, jungle-lined waterway, Reynolds was unaware that 150 kilometres away the Berhala and Bangka Straits were littered with the corpses of those who had sailed from Singapore on that fateful Friday 13 February 1942.

CHAPTER THREE

Black Friday

The languid, tropical peace of the Indragiri River was completely at odds with the hideous carnage taking place just over the horizon. A little-used highway linking the heart of Sumatra's jungle-covered interior to the sea, the river flowed lazily, passing through almost impenetrable rainforest before finally disgorging itself via a myriad of channels into the Berhala Straits. Downstream, it was an artist's delight, the dark, sombre tones of mangrove-dotted islands providing a perfect foil for the masses of mauve water hyacinths. Upriver, away from the wide, open estuary and the fishing village of Prigi Radja, the somewhat forbidding nature of the narrowing waterway was relieved by shafts of light, filtered and diffused by the density of the jungle canopy. Beyond the muddy banks, the lush foliage stretched endlessly, interupted only by the purple, mist-enshrouded peaks of distant mountains.

Such was the Indragiri's remoteness that the few visitors who ventured into this untamed wilderness might have imagined themselves to be alone, had it not been for the occasional fisherman or a solitary crocodile floating motionless in the shallows. Until the events of 14 February 1942 suddenly intruded upon their sheltered world, life for the few villagers who dwelt in small settlements dotted along the banks had been one of peace and plenty, a time of harmonious co-existence between themselves and nature.

The first real indication that something was amiss was the sound of distant, heavy gunfire and columns of smoke smudging the horizon. What this meant was not known until the first survivors arrived at Prigi Radja, telling garbled tales of terror and death, and of large numbers of people clinging to wreckage in the sea and others stranded on various islands off the coast. However, with the communication along the river erratic at the best of times, it was not until late on February 15 that the Dutch Controller at Rengat, 100 kilometres upstream, learned of the enormity of the disaster. From the Durian Straits in the north to Bangka in the south, scores of Allied craft had been attacked by Japanese bombers and surface vessels. It was reported that such was the ferocity of one engagement near the island of Pompong, about 210 kilometres away, that hundreds of survivors, many in an appalling state, required immediate assistance.

Controller van Brenkel and his staff were still deciding what to do when, at ten o'clock that evening, Bill Reynolds turned up with *Kofuku Maru*'s fifty refugees — those on board *Silver Gull* having completed the last fifty kilometres from Chenko by lorry. Despite being forced to sail by night almost all the way, the voyage had been uneventful and *Kofuku Maru* had made the journey without mishap. The passengers too were in fine shape, considering that they had spent the last two days in extremely cramped and uncomfortable conditions. Not so lucky, they learned, was a mixed convoy of evacuees, which had left Tandjung Pinang twenty-four hours after Reynolds. Of the nine vessels, of which four were under tow, it appears that only one — a commandeered Chinese boat crewed by a handful of Australians — had made the crossing safely. The Australian soldiers were even more lucky to be alive than they could have imagined. About thirty of their countrymen who had arrived in Tandjung Pinang too late to be evacuated were later captured and massacred by the Japanese.

On learning of the plight of the castaways at Pompong and that an escape route through Sumatra had been opened up by British officers, Reynolds volunteered to mount a rescue operation. Completely disregarding the fact that to reach Pompong would necessitate his negotiating 110 kilometres of enemy-controlled waters, Reynolds enlisted the aid of the Dutch to round up fuel, mattresses, blankets and foodstuff. Stocked

Black Friday

with provisions *Kofuku Maru* and her crew, to which Reynolds had temporarily recruited Ipoh planter Paddy Jackson and a Royal Naval reservist, set off downstream at two o'clock on the morning of February 16. At 3 am the following day, after an exasperating twenty-five hour voyage — which had seen them stuck fast on one of the Indragiri's mudbanks for six hours after taking an ill-advised shortcut, and then almost colliding with a small Dutch trader, the *Tandjung Pinang* — they reached Pompong Island.

Three and a half hours later, the first rays of the sun revealed a shoreline littered with wreckage, much of it charred and splintered — a grim testimony to the events which had so recently taken place. Off one end of the island was the wreck of the *Kuala*, her superstructure poking pathetically from the water, while nearby was another mast, all that was to be seen of *Tien Kuang*, which had been scuttled in a vain effort to deter enemy aircraft from dropping further bombs on the island. Of *Kung Wo*, the third ship in this convoy, there was no sign at all.

The latter, which had arrived from Singapore within hours of the others, on February 14, had been the first to be attacked. Many of the passengers who had survived the initial onslaught had abandoned the badly damaged ship, only to be swept away and drowned by the ferocious tidal movements that swirled around the islands. While the remainder had gathered on Bengku Island wondering what to do next, *Tien Kuang* and *Kuala* had anchored off Pompong Island, about three kilometres away.

Unaware of the fate of *Kung Wo*, the ships' captains dispatched two boatloads of volunteers to go ashore and collect foliage with which to camouflage the vessels, now sheltering in the shadow of the island. The working parties had scarcely left the ships when the enemy bombers returned to finish off *Kung Wo*. Under attack from nine aircraft, the already crippled ship sank almost immediately. The enemy, spying the other two ships, had then mounted a concentrated attack, before turning its attention to survivors who, having jumped into the sea, were attempting to reach the safety of Pompong.

On board the stricken vessels, all hell had broken loose. Shrieks of the injured mingled with the hiss of escaping steam, only to be drowned out by deafening explosions as bomb after bomb slammed into the iron decking and superstructure.

Oblivious to their own safety, medical staff who were still able to function worked feverishly, trying to sort out those who could be saved from those who had no chance of survival, while sailors tried to assess the damage. As fires began to take hold, the stupidity of replacing trained Malay and Chinese personnel with Europeans became apparent. With no idea what to do and no knowledge of the layout of the ships, the substitute crews were completely useless as a firefighting force. As the tempo of the bombing and strafing increased and the smoke became more dense, many leapt into the sea, only to be caught by the current and drowned. Those who ultimately survived were amongst the last to leave. Cowering in perforated lifeboats and clinging to anything that could float, they made their way to Pompong Island where they were helped ashore by the stunned working parties who had watched, helpless, as the Japanese had attacked.

That some of these survivors were still alive was nothing short of miraculous. Marjorie de Malmanche, an English nurse who had been one of the last to leave *Kuala*, had slid down a rope into the sea to find that the only boat in sight, already crammed full, was surrounded by dozens of people clinging to the sides.

> 'I made for it and hung on with the others. There was only one oar, which was being used, not very effectively, by an elderly woman. I saw the two doctors [Australian Marjorie Lyon and Englishwoman Elsie Crowe] sliding down into the sea.'

As the heavily laden boat had made its way with agonising slowness towards Pompong Island, the bombers had begun to concentrate their attack on *Tien Kuang*. Terrified, Marjorie and the others had watched as many of those swimming in the water were blown to bits. One of the planes then turned its attention to the hopelessly overcrowded lifeboat.

> 'There was an unpleasant whistling sound, and, looking up, I saw a bomb falling straight for us. We all cringed towards the side of the boat, and the next minute were caught up in a huge wave which flung us onto the rocky beach of the island. Everybody scrambled over the rocks

and ran up the steeply wooded hillside. Halfway up, the planes came again, and we crouched behind the trees for protection. Bombs fell, and our boat and the rocks went up in smoke.'

When the aircraft had finally departed, a number of men had returned to *Tien Kuang*, stripping her of everything of value. Hoping that by sinking her the Japanese would bother them no further, they opened the seacocks, only to discover a short time later, when the aircraft returned to strafe the beach, that it had been a waste of time.

About seven hundred of the original one thousand passengers had been marooned on Bengku and Pompong Islands. With little food or water and virtually nothing in the way of medical supplies most would have perished had not some of them, with the aid of local fishermen, managed to raise the alarm. Help, however, was a long time coming in these thinly populated islands and it was not for two or three days that the first rescue boats, sent north from Singkep Island by local chieftain Amir Silahili, reached Pompong and Bengku. By the time Bill Reynolds learned that help was needed, many of the more able-bodied had been rescued and taken to Singkep. From here they were eventually ferried to the escape routes operating along the Djambi and Indragiri Rivers, where they joined hundreds of other castaways who owed their lives either to a shuttle service run by Chinese and Malay fishermen or to the outstanding courage and tenacity of individuals who were determined that they would survive. (See Appendix II.)

Others who, having been rescued, tried to outrun enemy naval guns further to the south, were not as fortunate. After dropping off at the Indragiri River about half of the 208 women and children she had rescued from Pompong in the early hours of February 17, *Tandjung Pinang* (the ship that had almost collided with *Kofuku Maru*) had continued on to Java. Late on the night of the 18th she had been caught in a searchlight beam and attacked. There were only eleven survivors, all of whom took to a makeshift life raft. Five days later, only five were left alive and of these, only one, Englishwoman Molly Watts-Carter, who was later picked up by a Japanese cruiser, was known to have survived.

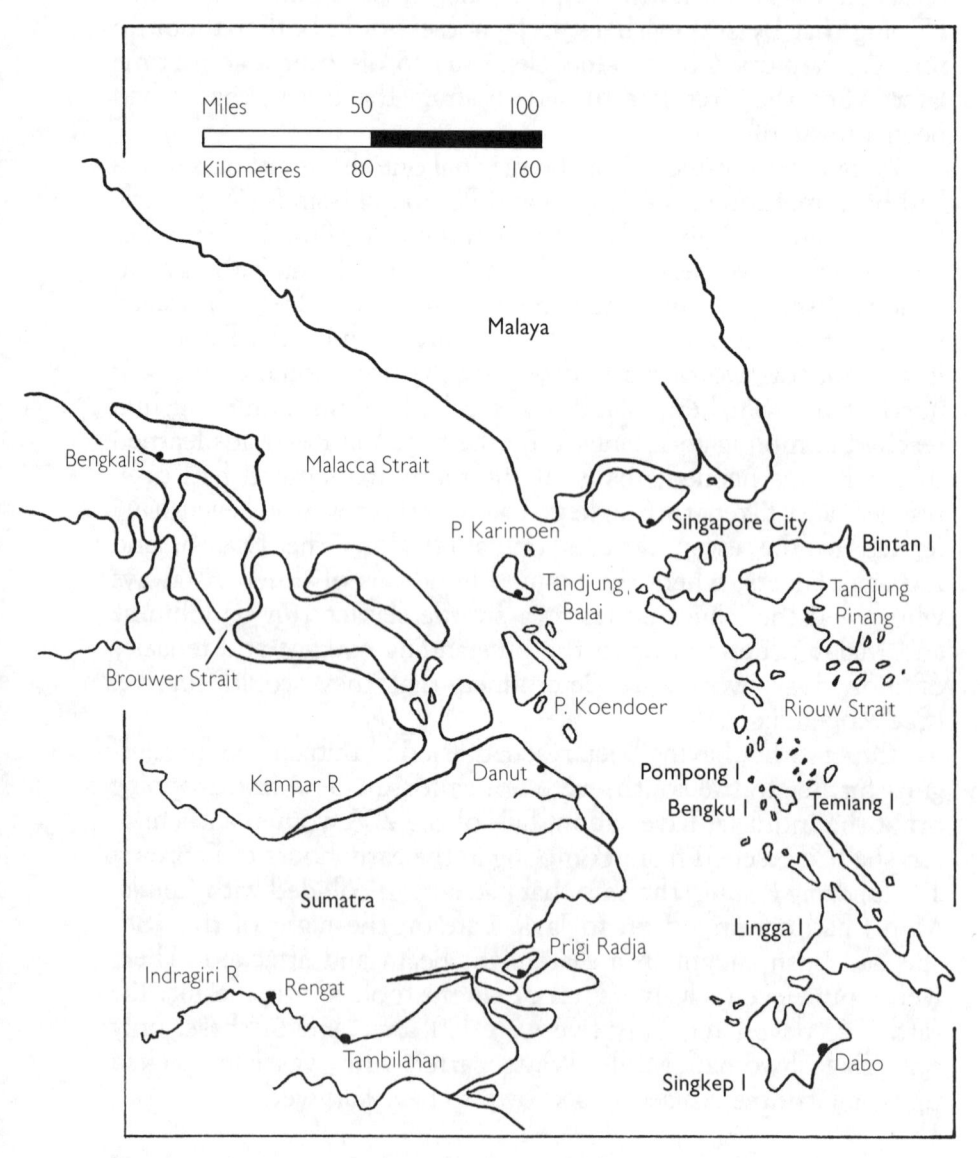

Map 1. The Escape Route from Singapore to the Indragiri River.

As he made his way ashore at Pompong in the pale dawn light, Reynolds, now sporting a bushy grey beard that gave him the air of a geriatric pirate, could see several figures tending the wounded in a roughly constructed first-aid post. Judging from the stench of rotting flesh born on the early morning air it was evident that, had help not arrived, more mounds of newly turned sand, topped by crude wooden crosses, would have added to those already ranged in rows along the narrow beach. Indeed, had it not been for the tireless efforts of medical staff, particularly Australians Doctor Marjorie Lyon, who was herself wounded, and Sister G. Dowling, the death toll would have been even higher. With the assistance of a number of English nursing staff including Marjorie de Malmanche and Brenda Macduff (a Sister from Malaya's Tanjung Batu Hospital who was well known to Reynolds), they had managed, with the most rudimentary equipment and only basic medical supplies, to keep alive a number of people who would have otherwise been long since dead.

Realising that it would be too risky to attempt to evacuate these seriously wounded people until nightfall, Reynolds sailed around the opposite side of the island where the main camp had been set up near a small permanent spring. To the horror of the four hundred or so castaways who had been anxiously scanning the horizon ever since the departure of the *Tandjung Pinang*, *Kofuku Maru* came into view at the same time as a Japanese plane flew overhead. However, to everyone's relief, the familiar shape of the fishing vessel evidently reassured the pilot, as no attack was made. Promising the hundreds who had to remain behind that he would come back as soon as possible, Reynolds took on a small number of women and the less seriously wounded before leaving to pick up the gravely ill from the makeshift hospital on the sandy beach. Even with the tireless assistance of the nursing staff, it was not until midnight that Reynolds and his seventy-six refugees, nine of whom were hideously injured, were able to head for the safety of the Indragiri River.

The voyage, referred to by Reynolds as 'shuffling' and by Sister Brenda Macduff as 'very uncomfortable', would probably have been more accurately described as a nightmare.

With no accommodation other than *Kofuku Maru*'s bare boards, and with little or no protection at night from the cool monsoon wind or the scorching sun the following day, the evacuees were sardined into two small areas of decking, which were strewn with an assortment of ropes, gear, chains and miscellaneous junk. So cramped were the conditions that the able-bodied had to take turns to stand up and stretch their legs. There was no queue to make use of the lone bucket on the rope — the passengers were so dehydrated and undernourished that no one needed to use it.

Fifteen weary hours after their departure from Pompong, Reynolds finally nosed his ship alongside a rickety jetty at Tambilahan, a tiny settlement that lay between Prigi Radja and Rengat. While the uninjured moved on to more comfortable accommodation for the journey further upstream, Reynolds renewed his brief acquaintance with an Australian doctor, a surgical wizard by the name of Albert (Bertie) Coates, who had turned a small native clinic into a hospital.

A lieutenant-colonel from the 10th Australian General Hospital in Malaya, Coates had left Singapore on the evacuation ship *Sui Kwong* at around midnight on February 13, only to be shipwrecked sixteen hours later when the Japanese bombed the vessel. By great good fortune, Coates, one of Australia's finest surgeons, had been rescued by *Tengorah* — a luxury launch belonging to the Sultan of Johore which had been used to evacuate a number of senior Allied personnel, including Coates's fellow countryman, Colonel Broadbent.

When the first of the wounded had been put ashore at Tambilahan on February 15, Coates had remained with them, taking over the small dispensary as an aid post and rejecting all suggestions that he should flee to safety while there was still time. Just on dusk four days later, when *Kofuku Maru* turned up from Pompong, he was roused from his work by the sound of Bill Reynolds's distinctively Australian voice bellowing from the water 'Colonel Coates! Here is a new load of customers, plenty of them. Get your saw sharpened up'. That night, after the patients had been manhandled with great difficulty off the ship and up the spidery steps of the jetty, they were taken to a primitive room euphemistically called an 'operating theatre'. Here Bertie Coates, using the most basic surgical instruments (one of which was a chopper donated by a local), performed seven major operations.

Reynolds, however, did not hang around to witness the miraculous surgery performed by Coates. As soon as the last patient had left the ship and the rest were all assigned to other vessels for the trip to Rengat, he was off again to Pompong where he discovered that the arrival of three Malay *tonkans* in his absence had reduced the number of evacuees by two-thirds. Among the ninety-six people now anxiously awaiting *Kofuku Maru*'s return were Singapore's Public Works Departmental Head, Mr Nunn, and his wife. Having refused to be parted from her husband, Mrs Nunn was the only woman left on the island.

For the next eight days Reynolds did not pause to rest. Learning from the reports that were still flooding in that there were many others awaiting rescue, he set sail for other islands of the archipelago, visiting in turn Moro village on Sugibawah Island, then Bengku, Singkep, Pompong and Lingga Islands to collect stragglers rounded up by Malay fishermen. His decision, since *Kofuku Maru* was so obviously a Japanese vessel, to sail under Chinese colours reassured the locals, who pulled out all stops to help him. By the time he had finished his work, the co-operation of the local people would ensure that Reynolds would rescue no less than 1519 people. Flying the Chinese flag, *Kofuku Maru*, under the able command of William Roy Reynolds, had become an integral part of the Allied escape route.

It was while returning from one of these missions, on about February 24, that Reynolds noticed a small sailing craft negotiating the waters of the Indragiri's estuary. Thinking that the two occupants might require a tow, or perhaps wish to be picked up, he altered course.

As *Kofuku Maru* came alongside, her wash adding to the chop on the water, Reynolds and his passengers were startled to see a figure, shorts around its ankles, pitch headlong over the side of the boat. Seconds later and much to the amusement of the boat's other occupant, as well as *Kofuku Maru*'s now very interested gallery, a head emerged, spluttering waterlogged curses in tones that were obviously Welsh. Mustering what dignity he had left, a very wet Welshman, now minus the shorts into which he had been changing at the time of Reynolds's inopportune arrival, clambered back on board. Meantime his companion, a captain in the Gordon Highlanders, assured Reynolds that they were perfectly all right and were making for Prigi Radja, where they intended to find a powered boat to take them on to Rengat. Satisfied that the Gordon had the matter well in hand, Reynolds resumed his journey up river.

Some hours later, he had just finished securing *Kofuku Maru* to the wharf at Rengat when he heard the sound of a small diesel engine followed by a bump as the ship rocked on her mooring lines. Never one to suffer fools gladly, particularly in all matters pertaining to the sea, Bill Reynolds stormed out of the wheelhouse.

Even without his beard, the two metre tall, mahogany-tanned figure clad in a pair of filthy shorts and a tattered shirt was a most intimidating sight. Without waiting to see who or what was responsible, Reynolds let forth a stream of colourful invectives which, after years of practice, with the sea, he had refined to an art form. So fluent was his abuse, much of it delivered in the earthy style of the Australian vernacular, that in the two-minute tirade did not repeat himself once. With his spleen finally vented, he glared through his horn-rimmed spectacles to see who was responsible for this exhibition of outrageously poor seamanship. To his astonishment he discovered that the object of his tirade was the Gordon Highlander whom he had met on the Indragiri estuary that very morning. To his further amazement he saw that, far from being reduced to a mass of quivering jelly by the vitriolic outburst, the officer could scarcely contain his mirth. Bill Reynolds had finally met his match.

Twenty-seven-year-old Captain Ivan Lyon introduced himself and his companion, Corporal Ron 'Taffy' Morris, who was now decently clad in another pair of shorts. With the introductions over and Reynolds's outburst reduced to a mere trickle, Lyon suggested that with the sun well over the yardarm it was high time for a drink — thereby dissolving any vestige of animosity that Reynolds may have felt inclined to harbour. It was over this very congenial tipple that Reynolds discovered Ivan Lyon was a man after his own heart.

Although a professional soldier and a graduate of Sandhurst Military College who had volunteered for service with his regiment in Singapore in 1937, the Englishman was not quite what he appeared. Before the outbreak of hostilities with Japan he had been seconded from normal duties to join a clandestine, highly irregular operation, whose main aim had been to bump-off Japanese agents operating in Malaya and Siam (now Thailand). Furthermore, Lyon's first love was not the land but the sea and, despite his unfortunate mishap a few minutes earlier, he was an expert single-handed yachtsman with extensive knowledge of local waters. Indeed, it was Lyon's seafaring ability, as much as his fluency in Malay and undercover experience, which had resulted in his being sent from Singapore on February 2 to organise a route to transport materials and men from India, through Sumatra and on to Singapore. Although the initial concept had been to initiate and keep open a supply route in the event of a prolonged siege, the plan had been amended when it was realised that any movement would be out of, rather than into, Singapore.

It was the formation of this escape route that had been responsible for bringing Reynolds and Lyon together. The Australian, who up until now had only a vague idea of how the route worked, learned of the complex organisation that had been required to set it up. Lyon's role, assisted by Morris, an orderly with the Royal Army Medical Corps, had been to establish a base and supply dump on uninhabited Durian Island, at the head of the Durian Strait. From here they had directed shipwreck survivors and refugees rounded up by a network of local fishermen to Prigi Radja, where Lyon's colleague Major Jock Campbell had been waiting. While Lyon liaised with the local chieftains, Campbell, a former planter, had used his organisational skills to establish staging posts up the river to Rengat, where refugees had then been transported by a variety of means across the mountains to Padang, on Sumatra's west coast. Once safely at Padang, evacuation by Allied vessels had proved to be comparatively easy.

Although this route across the mountains, the one which Lyon, Morris and Campbell would shortly take, was accepted as being the only one open to the west and freedom, Reynolds had other plans. He informed Lyon that when the time came to quit the Indragiri, he intended to sail *Kofuku Maru* across the Indian Ocean to India via the enemy-infested Malacca Straits. It was for this very reason that he had been stockpiling fuel for days, always taking on board a little more than he needed.

It was now Lyon's turn to listen, and he did so with mounting excitement. When the Australian pointed out that *Kofuku Maru* had been crisscrossing Japanese-controlled waters unmolested for the best part of two weeks, a plan that had been formulating in the recesses of Lyon's mind suddenly crystalised. If *Kofuku Maru* could get out of Singapore without any trouble, she could also get back in.

Within minutes Lyon and Reynolds had made a pact. Provided both survived, they would meet again in Bombay.

CHAPTER FOUR

The Amazing Voyage of the *Suey Sin Fah*

Leaving Lyon and Morris to make arrangements with Campbell to travel overland to Rengat, Reynolds once again set off down the Indragiri in search of survivors. Although hundreds of castaways had been more than ready to board the ship when they needed to, Reynolds found it ironic that so far he had not had any luck in persuading a single soul to come with him across the Indian Ocean. Not even the outrageous rumour that *Kofuku Maru*, being a spy ship, was filled with sophisticated equipment, swelled the ranks — although Colonel Coates, who was now in Rengat with his patients awaiting transport to Padang, and a British officer, Colonel Dillon (both of whom had no illusions about the ship), had been sorely tempted. Earlier that day Coates had explained that while he was more than pleased to accept Reynolds's gifts of tobacco, gin and slouch hat and to treat a neck injury for crewman Ah Tee, he could not take up the offer to sail to India as he could not leave his patients. Dillon, who was responsible for the well-being of his men, also reluctantly declined the opportunity to join the Australian, whom he later fondly described as 'a real old pirate'.

On March 6, when the number of evacuees coming up the Indragiri had been reduced to a trickle, the Dutch asked Reynolds if he would be willing to indulge in a spot of espionage while dropping off emergency food supplies to an outlying community. Notwithstanding the probability that Sumatra and the rest of the East Indies would soon fall to the Japanese, Reynolds, with no misgivings whatsoever, acceded to this request. As soon as the necessary paperwork was completed he took on 119 sacks of rice and headed for the Riouw Archipelago.

It was perhaps in deference to his Chinese companions that Reynolds at this point decided to rename the ship. Although *Kofuku Maru* meant 'happiness', it can hardly have been popular with the Chinese who, apart from being longtime and bitter enemies of the Japanese, were highly superstitious. Inspired by the nature of his mission and the masses of water hyacinths growing in such profusion that at times they blocked the lower reaches of the Indragiri, Reynolds discarded the Nipponese name in favour of British Privateer *Suey Sin Fah*. Despite its rather swashbuckling English prefix, the remainder of the title, being Chinese for 'a star-shaped water flower', pleased the crew, who considered it to be far better 'joss'.

Although the voyage from the mouth of the Indragiri across the Berhala Straits passed without incident, Reynolds ran into serious trouble in the Riouw Straits. Challenged by a Japanese patrol boat near Tandjung Pinang, *Suey Sin Fah* was forced to make a fight of it. With the aid of a Lewis gun, Thompson machine guns and rifles, which Reynolds had had the foresight to acquire, the small fishing boat came off best in the altercation, eventually forcing the enemy vessel to flee to a small strait which lay to the south.

Instead of putting as much distance between himself and potential trouble as possible, Reynolds, exhilarated by the incident, stuck to his agreed route and sailed deeper into enemy territory to Tandjung Bali on Karimoen Island, which was within spitting distance of Singapore. Although he was quite unfazed by the encounter with the Japanese patrol boat, which had resulted in the ship being peppered with automatic fire, his Chinese crew was of a different mind. Every one of them deserted at the next port of call, Tandjung Batu on Pulau Koendoer, where there was a large Chinese community.

Although he now had only Elliott and Papworth to help him handle the ship, Reynolds, in his role as master spy, decided to return to the Indragiri via Dabo, on Singkep Island — a plan that was hastily amended when it was discovered that the Japanese were already in residence there. However, at the northern part of the island he was able to evacuate 120 Chinese women and children from a hospital before continuing up the Berhala Strait, where he collected together nine small boats containing mostly military personnel. Unfortunately, before the small flotilla reached the safety of the Indragiri estuary, the Japanese attacked, sinking eight of the small boats and forcing the ninth to run aground. Although *Suey Sin Fah* was undamaged, Reynolds sustained wounds to his feet and legs. When he finally reached Rengat he learned that, with the Japanese rapidly advancing, this trip — his tenth — had been his last.

While he and his exhausted crew rested, repairs were carried out on *Suey*'s stern, which had been rammed by the motor vessel *Pearlfisher* — an incident that undoubtedly had Reynolds voicing the odd colourful word or two. Fortunately, the repairs were almost completed when the Controller's secretary, Mr Kaag, arrived on the afternoon of March 12 with the information that the Japanese were heading north up the Djambi River valley and were expected to reach Rengat within forty-eight hours.

Clearly, it was high time to leave. However, in order to ensure all those heading downriver had a head start, it was decided to blow up all water craft still left in Rengat. Explosives were placed on more than sixty vessels, which ranged from *Tengorah*, the Sultan's luxurious motor launch, to an almost brand new Catalina tanker which had been taken from a RAF base at Blakang Mati Island and which was filled with high octane spirit. Only one boat was saved from what must have been a most spectacular conflagration. The most lowly of the lot, she was a three-metre dingy named *Supply* — a name long associated with Australian maritime history. As Reynolds loaded her on board *Suey Sin Fah*, he noted with admiration that the tiny craft, in common with her namesake which had voyaged from England to Australia in 1787, had been sailed all the way from Singapore by a bunch of very 'tough guys'.

With the demolition work successfully completed, Reynolds applied himself to the task of augmenting his sadly depleted crew. Apparently there were few European applicants, since three of the four newcomers were Chinese. Filling the role of stewardess/cook/deputy helmsperson was a remarkable young woman, Cantonese-born Looi Pek Sye, who had escaped from Ipoh,

The first entry in the Log of the British Privateer *Suey Sin Fah*, 12 March 1942.

Rengat, Indragiri towards Singkep, Sumatra

19.2.2[?]

Remarks

Alongside wharf at Rengat completing repairs to after taffrail, and towing chalice, occasioned by M/V "Pearlfisher" ramming our stern. During the day the Secretary to Resident advises that we leave for the open sea as Japanese troops are advancing from Djambi, and he fears that the town will be occupied within 48 hrs. Secure clearance for British India. During the day, at his request, ship as A/B, one Trant McNeil, R.N., acting Sick Berth Attendant, from Singkep Island refugee party. During the day take in dinghy, and dory, which rest and secure on fore deck. 7.15 pm Cast off moorings, swing, and proceed downstream, assisted by first ammang. Tide at young ebb.

8.30 pm Seaman McNeil reports having fallen and injured pelvis. Make for Chenako in order to land him and send to Rengat Hospital, in the meantime making comfortable on engine room skylight. He appears to be in great pain as a result of fall. 9.33 pm Alongside jetty at Chenako: helm and engines to M/o. Telephone Doctor at Rengat, who advises road impassable owing to flood water, and directs that patient be taken to Tambelihan. 11 pm Cast off moorings, swing, and proceed downstream at full speed. Patient appears much easier. Tide at last of ebb.

Malaya, with her three-year-old daughter, Lam Kwai (Twin Seasons). Two men, thirty-four-year-old Ah Kwai from Tien Tsin and thirty-two-year-old Ah Chung, from Shanghai, were to act as motormen. After obtaining clearance from British Headquarters in India, Reynolds also took on as a sick-berth attendant, Frank McNeil RN, a twenty-three-year-old Londoner who had arrived with a party of refugees from Singkep.

At 7.30 that evening, with the assistance of Pilot Amman, *Suey Sin Fah* slipped her moorings and set off downriver on the ebb tide. However, just over an hour later, McNeil began to have second thoughts about the wisdom of undertaking such a trip. Telling Reynolds that he had fallen and injured his pelvis, he put on such a convincing performance of being in excruciating pain that Reynolds immobilised him on the roof of the engine-room housing and made for the nearest telephone, which they found in the village of Chenko. Ninety minutes later, with McNeil still on board, they were heading downstream once more. After finally raising a doctor, Reynolds had learned that the overland track back to Rengat was impassable due to local flooding and that the patient would have to be taken to Tambilahan.

It was after 5 am before McNeil, lying prostrate on a stretcher carried by Elliott and Papworth, finally reached hospital. Three hours later, to Reynolds's utter astonishment, he reappeared, walking under his own steam and exhibiting no sign of the pain which had afflicted him such a short time previously. During the subsequent interview, acerbicly described by Reynolds as a 'cross-examination', McNeil admitted that he had feigned illness as he considered only madmen would attempt such a voyage. Reynolds, who was himself suffering some discomfort from the injuries to his feet and legs, was livid. After a few choice words, the mildest of which was 'coward', Reynolds dismissed McNeil and arranged for him to be taken back to Rengat at the earliest opportunity. As things turned out the malingerer should have stayed with the lunatics for, within hours of his return to Rengat, the Japanese arrived.

Having made such a fast trip downriver, Reynolds now had plenty of time to ensure that the ship was ready for her journey across the open sea. For the rest of that day, Friday March 13, and for the whole of the next, he and the ship's company were busy. While the crew bunkered oil, stowed gear and secured to the foremast gaff and boom a lifeboat sail belonging to the ill-fated *Kuala*, Reynolds visited the hospital to have his injuries dressed before adjourning to the Controller's office to catch up on the latest military intelligence.

The news that had come through was not reassuring. Although there were reports of sporadic guerilla fighting, the enemy now occupied many key centres in Sumatra. The Dutch had surrendered Padang without a fight, trapping thousands of escape route refugees. Reynolds knew that in order to avoid a similar fate, he should clear out immediately while he still had the chance.

Just after seven o'clock on the morning of Sunday March 15 *Suey Sin Fah*, with Pilot Amman on board, left Tambilahan for the last time. Stopping off at Prigi Radja only long enough for the pilot to leap onto the jetty, Reynolds, without any charts and no instruments other than a compass, headed for northern Sumatra. That night, believing that a Dutch minefield was ahead, he anchored off Danut village only to find, after half an hour's cautious creeping inshore the following morning, that there was no evidence whatsoever of any minefield. Resuming full speed, they then had a trouble-free run across smooth seas to Sungei Pakning village where the ship anchored for the night. Although the local Malays were surly and uncommunicative, the Chinese from the village were very friendly and readily imparted some local intelligence. They informed Reynolds that low-flying aircraft had been visiting the port on a daily basis and had strafed Allied soldiers on the Sungei Siak estuary on March 11.

Although they reported that no planes had been seen for two days, Reynolds did not dally long enough to determine whether this was still the case. Shortly after first light he left for Bengkalis. Two hours later, under the watchful eye of Controller Warnaar, he was tying up at the jetty. Although Warnaar would prove most helpful in facilitating their further passage, Reynolds knew the Controller's suggestion that *Suey Sin Fah* proceed at once to Began-Siapiapi and hide among the Chinese fishing vessels was motivated more by a desire to be rid of them before the Japanese arrived than any deep concern for their well-being. Much to Warnaar's consternation, Reynolds elected to remain in port, resting the crew, cleaning the engine

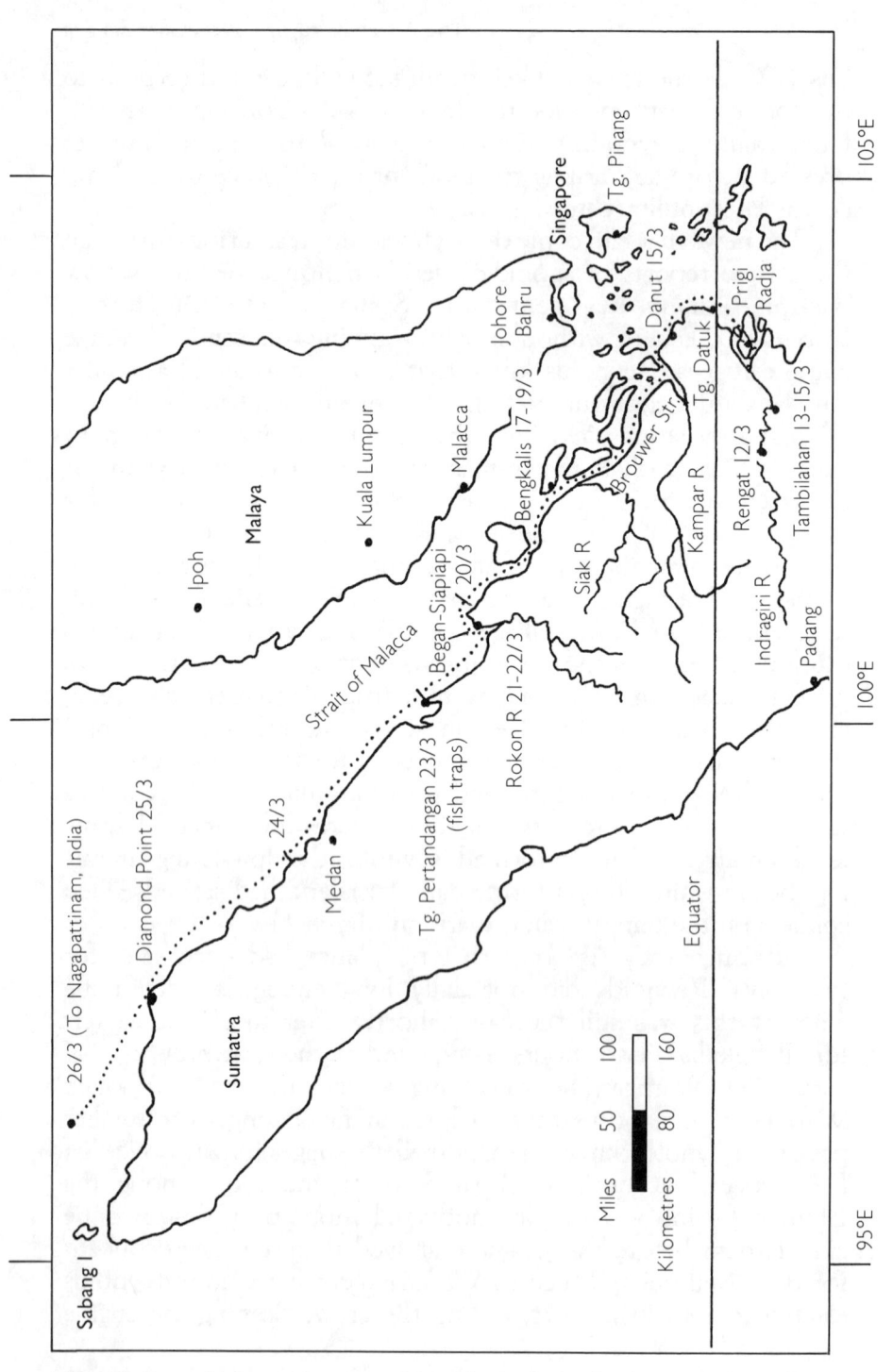

Map II. Reynolds's escape route from the Indragiri River.

The Amazing Voyage of the *Suey Sin Fah*

and checking that the machine guns and rifles were in order.

It was evidently the size of *Suey Sin Fah*'s arsenal that prompted the Dutchman, late in the afternoon of March 17, to ask Reynolds what he intended to do if enemy craft entered the harbour. Reynolds's reply that he 'would engage them in action' was the last thing that the Controller, who had hopes of negotiating with the Japanese, wanted to hear. In the 'heated discussion' which followed, Reynolds reluctantly agreed that if he wanted to shoot at the enemy he would not do so inshore but would sail out into the Brouwer Strait. Although this was merely a narrow strip of sea separating the island of Bengkalis from Sumatra, it was evidently sufficiently removed from Dutch territory to be regarded as international waters. With exceedingly bad grace, Reynolds also promised that he would not fire at enemy aircraft while in port.

During the night, motormen Ah Kwai and Ah Chung deserted. At eight o'clock the next evening, a very nervous Controller, whose anxiety over the appearance of an enemy reconnaissance plane that morning had been increased tenfold by the news that Japanese troops would shortly be advancing down the Siak River to take Bengkalis, ordered Reynolds to leave by midnight. The mere thought of *Suey Sin Fah* being captured in a Dutch port was one that the Dutchman clearly preferred not to contemplate, 'an armed merchant ship being difficult to explain away'.

Reynolds, who was quite prepared to accede to this not unreasonable request, was prevented from leaving when a violent tropical storm, known as a 'Sumatra', blew up out of nowhere. Although the problem of a lack of motormen had been solved by Reynolds's gaining the services of two Malays in exchange for towing the motor launch *Rasak* to Began-Siapiapi, heavy seas delayed their departure until early the next evening, March 19.

By dawn the following day they had left Bengkalis far behind and entered the mangrove-lined Allah Muda Creek, where they hid alongside a charcoal burner's jetty until nightfall. The decision to keep out of sight was a wise one, for at 11 am a reconnaissance aircraft flew over, causing them to assume action stations. Luckily, they had not been detected and, under cover of darkness, they proceeded to the old pirate haunt of Began-Siapiapi, which they reached shortly after 8 am on March 21. Here Reynolds took on oil and stores and engaged two Malays, one to act as motorman and the other — a seventeen-year-old youth from Kuala Lumpur named Saitaan bin Abdulhamid — to fill the role of deckhand.

The sight of the armed British Privateer *Suey Sin Fah* did not meet with the approval of this Controller either, for later that evening he politely suggested that they should leave as soon as it was convenient. Reynolds, who did not usually take kindly to being told what to do by anyone, did not take umbrage at this request, since he had learned that Japanese occupation of the town was only days away. The only reason it had escaped the attentions of the enemy so far was that control of the large Chinese population of 25 000 required a substantial enemy garrison. Sufficient troops were being landed to ensure that it, too, would soon be under Japanese control.

Although Reynolds had not gone so far as to commit himself to a departure time, the matter was taken out of his hands the next day. Shortly after a visit by a reconnaissance plane, Controller Vischer told Reynolds that as all communications with the Dutch Resident in Rengat had been cut, he should leave posthaste. He was just about to do so when the police inspector arrived and forcibly removed the newly acquired motorman on the pretext that he was wanted by his wife for desertion. Reynolds was back to square one.

Anxious to be rid of *Suey Sin Fah*, which was regarded as a distinct liability, the police supplied a mechanic to start the engine — a complicated procedure which involved the use of compressed air. Having been informed that the Japanese would be in town by morning, Vischer insisted that the ship leave immediately, giving Reynolds no other option but to appoint Elliott to take charge of the engine. It was not until 9.30 pm on March 22 that they finally left their mooring at the mouth of the Rokon River, much to the Controller's relief.

Knowing that it would be fatal at this point to arouse the suspicions of Japanese aircraft that constantly patrolled the skies, Reynolds and his crew were compelled to exercise caution as they left Began-Siapiapi. For the next two nights they continued their policy of sailing only under cover of darkness, anchoring by day near one of the many native fishing traps that jutted out into

The Amazing Voyage of the *Suey Sin Fah*

the water from the coastal village of Tandjung Pertandangan. With *Kuala*'s lifeboat sail hoisted and the ship stationary beside the fishing stakes, they looked for all the world like innocent fishermen going about their normal business. The ruse obviously worked since, although enemy aircraft were seen, none came down for a closer look. The fishermen, whose traps they had temporarily borrowed, kept them up to date with the movements of the Japanese, who were by now occupying every large centre.

Aided by generally fine weather and a favourable current, *Suey Sin Fah* made good progress. By March 24 they had cleared the Malacca Straits and, evidently out of the area being patrolled by the Japanese, were no longer forced to hide during daylight. The following day they were off Diamond Point, on Sumatra's northerly tip and the next day were well into the Indian Ocean, steaming towards Nagapattinam in southern India at a rate of about eight knots. Other than the glow from fishermen's fires burning in Mus village, which they noticed as they passed to the north of the Nicobar Islands, they saw no sign of life and nothing whatsoever of any interest. Indeed, from March 25 onwards Reynolds's log, written in meticulously neat handwriting in three thin exercise books, made very boring reading, with the repetitious 'fine/clear/cloudy, smooth/slight/choppy, no enemy aircraft' entries giving way to the even briefer 'similar weather conditions' as they chugged across the Indian Ocean.

At precisely twenty minutes to four o'clock on the afternoon of Tuesday March 31, sixteen days after leaving the Indragiri River, *Suey Sin Fah* dropped anchor in the Nagapattinam Roads. Reynolds, after a feat of amazing seamanship and navigation, which had found him only thirty-two kilometres out in his distance reckoning, had reached his destination. He was ordered ashore immediately by the Port Officer, who instructed him to board the five o'clock train for Madras, about 290 kilometres to the north, for debriefing by the Senior Naval Officer.

There was not the slightest risk of *Suey Sin Fah* disappearing while Reynolds was absent. With no air left in the starter bottles, and the compressor which was used to refill them defective, the engine could not be fired without outside assistance. When his interview was over, Reynolds returned to Nagapattinam, had the engine restarted and sailed the ship to the naval dockyard in

Madras for a complete overhaul. He had plenty of time, for it was not until the third week of April that Ivan Lyon appeared to fulfil his half of the pact made on the far-off Indragiri River.

Compared to Lyon's trip across the Indian Ocean, the voyage of the *Suey Sin Fah* had been a pleasure cruise. When Lyon, Morris and Campbell had left Rengat at the end of February, they had been subjected to a terrifying ride across the mountains in pitch darkness in the back of an open tourer, only to discover that the submarine which was to pick them up on the west coast had not kept the rendezvous. After considerable backtracking, they had reached Padang on March 2 to find the small town overflowing with refugees. Although many, including Morris, were evacuated to Ceylon in the next day or two, the number of ships reaching Padang decreased alarmingly, so much so that the senior Allied officer, who also happened to be Lyon's Commanding Officer, Colonel Alan Warren, had realised that almost all of those remaining would have little chance of escaping.

On March 8, with the Japanese within one hundred kilometres of the town, Warren had ordered Lyon, Campbell and sixteen others whose contribution to the war effort could be useful, to leave Sumatra on a native-style fishing boat or *prahu*, which he had secreted further up the coast. Not much more than a floating seedpod, *Sederhana Djohanes* was not an inspiring sight. Made entirely of hand-hewn wooden planks and with sails that were so rotten that a finger could be poked easily through them, she looked incapable of sailing across a pond, let alone across the ocean to India.

Yet, with only the most basic navigational aids — a page torn from a Sumatran pilot book, a radio with an inadequate supply of batteries, a prismatic compass and an unreliable wristwatch — Ivan Lyon, with the assistance of a merchant marine navigator, had brought the small ship safely across the ocean. It had not been an easy job. Dogged by weather that see-sawed from raging tempest to breathless calm, strafed by enemy aircraft and forced to exert his will on shipmates who at one stage wanted to surrender rather than continue, Lyon had exhibited bravery and resilience that far outstripped the limits of normal men. It was due almost entirely to him that after a 2656 kilometre voyage, lasting fifty-two days, *Sederhana Djohanes* had reached Ceylon.

It was not until much later that it was discovered just how lucky they had been to evade capture, or worse. All those trapped in Rengat, including Dr Bertie Coates, who had turned down Reynold's invitation to sail to India in order to stay with his patients, and Dr Marjorie Lyon and her nursing sisters who had saved so many lives at Pompong, spent the rest of the war behind barbed wire. Captured also was Colonel Dillon who, having passed up the chance to escape with Reynolds, managed to flee Padang in a small boat at the last minute, only to be intercepted off the coast of India by the Japanese. Others, whom Lyon and Reynolds had taken such pains to rescue from the islands of the Berhala Straits, were never seen again.

Rooseboom, a Dutch freighter filled with evacuees, some of whom were Reynolds's Pompong castaways, was one of the vessels that had not made it to safety. Torpedoed just off the Sumatran coast, she had sunk quickly, taking Mr Nunn and hundreds of others with her. The one lifeboat, at first jam-packed with survivors, had floated aimlessly for weeks until only four were left alive. Mrs Nunn, who had escaped the sinking vessel when her husband pushed her to safety through a porthole, was not one of them. Hideous as her suffering and death from starvation and exposure had been, Mrs Nunn was, perhaps, among the more fortunate. Many others, including the Argylls' unflappable Drummer Hardy, the last man to cross the causeway, died at the hands of a murderous band of English army deserters, who cannibalised their victims before their depraved activities were detected and they were forced over the side.

Unaware of the appalling fate which had overtaken so many in the waters of the Indian Ocean, Lyon wasted no time in locating Reynolds, who had been cooling his heels in Madras and Bombay for the best part of three weeks. Finding both the ship and his friend in one piece, Lyon outlined to Reynolds a plan he had evolved during the long hours that were spent at the tiller of the *Sederhana Djohanes*.

Essentially, it involved their sneaking back to Singapore Harbour with a group of highly trained men to secrete incendiary devices on shore-based installations and place delayed action limpet mines on the hulls of cargo vessels. *Suey Sin Fah*, in the guise of a Japanese fishing boat, would provide the transportation from India. While she hid in the mangroves of Sumatra's Kampar River estuary, the saboteurs would carry out the raid with the aid of small, collapsible two-man craft known as folboats. With a six-hour time fuse attached to the explosive devices, Lyon was confident that the raiders would be well away before the targets blew up.

This daring plan sounded perfectly feasible to Bill Reynolds. In 1925, shortly before he left the merchant marine, he had gone to Mecca disguised as an Arab — a stunt that would have cost the Infidel his life had his real identity been uncovered. Not surprisingly, Reynolds figured that if it were possible to enter Islam's most holy city in the guise of a Muslim pilgrim, it was perfectly logical to assume that Japanese defences could be penetrated by a Japanese fishing boat. Unfortunately, at this time, there were only two people who shared this viewpoint — himself and Ivan Lyon.

It was not until early May that Lyon, his list of contacts almost exhausted, finally found a sympathetic ear. With the co-operation of an old friend, Bernard Fergusson, Lyon by-passed army red tape to reach General Wavell, now based in Dehli. Wavell, whose willingness to try unorthodox ideas did not always meet with the approval of his more conservative colleagues, gave the plan his blessing — with one proviso. Knowing that, with the Indian Ocean, Burma and Malaya a hive of Japanese activity, the raid would have more chance of success if the approach to Singapore were made from the east, Wavell told Lyon that the operation would have to originate from Australia.

With Wavell's backing, the promise of funding from Special Operations in London and a letter of introduction in his pocket, Lyon began to set the wheels in motion. After securing the services of his escape route colleague, Jock Campbell, to assist in organisation, he travelled to Ceylon where, with some difficulty, he succeeded in extricating Taffy Morris from his post at a military hospital in Colombo. At the beginning of June, after making arrangements for Morris and Campbell to follow him to Australia on the next available ship, Lyon had a final meeting with Bill Reynolds.

Lyon and Reynolds, who was to sail *Suey Sin Fah* to Australia as soon as the overhaul on the engine was complete, each had

The Amazing Voyage of the *Suey Sin Fah*

one last task to perform before they parted company — Reynolds to re-christen the ship yet again and Lyon to devise a code name for the proposed operation. Neither had any problem with their respective choices. Reynolds settled on *Krait* (pronounced 'Krite') — a small but deadly Indian snake, whose ability to strike with unexpected and lightning rapidity was known to millions worldwide through the stories of writer Rudyard Kipling. From a metal craftsman he then ordered a copper replica of the snake, which was to be the ship's mascot. Evidently the artisan assigned to execute the work had either a very poor knowledge of Indian reptiles or an eye for the flamboyant. When Reynolds's order was finally delivered it was not a model of the innocuous-looking Krait that arrived but a miniature version of a hooded Cobra, brilliantly captured in the strike position. Such was the superb workmanship that Reynolds overlooked the fact that his mascot was entirely the wrong variety and gave it pride of place in the ship.

Lyon, whose motive for organising the raid was to lessen the loss of Singapore and the humiliating smell of defeat, chose for his operation the far more obscure 'Jay Wick' — an offbeat name that was chosen for very esoteric reasons. Contrary to post-war opinion that the tiny English port of Jaywick had prompted the name, Jay Wick originated not from East Anglia but the Far East. Besides its being a well known and powerful deodoriser used to sweeten the malodorous air of Singapore's public lavatories, the humble but indispensible Jaywick was the object of a long-standing private joke shared between Lyon and his close friend and sailing companion, Gordon Highlander Francis Moir-Byres.

Before the war, while exploring the coast of eastern Malaya in their yacht *Vinette*, the pair had been attempting to negotiate a series of sandbars in very rough conditions when a basket of eggs, suspended from the roof of the galley, had broken free. The fragile shells had smashed upon the floor into one great slimy mess, sliding into every nook and cranny before seeping into the bilge to rapidly decompose. In the oppressive tropical conditions below decks the stench had been so overpowering that for the rest of the voyage Ivan made sure that not a single day passed without his reminding a long-suffering Francis, 'If only we had a Jay Wick. That would get rid of the pong.'

Working on the assumption that if the magical Jay Wick could eliminate odours as repulsive as raw sewage and rotten eggs it could surely obliterate the stench of the British Empire's greatest military defeat, Lyon left his private joke for Francis and posterity. Provided all went according to plan, *Krait* would take Operation Jaywick to Singapore.

CHAPTER FIVE

A Plan Unfolds

To Ivan Lyon's consternation he discovered, shortly after his arrival in Australia, that he needed more than Wavell's letter to get Jaywick up and running. He had started out well enough, with most encouraging reactions during a meeting on July 4 with Fremantle's Naval Officer in Command, Commodore Collins, and the enthusiastic and controversial Australian general, H. Gordon Bennett. Heartening, too, had been his follow-up conference in Melbourne with Major Edgerton Mott, an English officer who had been seconded from British Special Operations to head a fledgling Australian equivalent.

Lyon's plan had enormous appeal for Mott. Like Bennett and Collins, who realised that Jaywick could be viable provided it had top-level support, he immediately contacted United States Intelligence to gain assistance from the all-powerful General Douglas MacArthur, now commanding Allied military operations in the South-West Pacific Area. To the utter dismay of both Mott and Lyon, Wavell's letter made no impression on MacArthur's influential underling, General Willoughby, who informed them that United States' plans for the future did not include Singapore.

Rebuffed by the Americans, they soon discovered that the Australian Army's attitude was not much better. Although interested in using the Jaywick concept in Timor, the AIF was unwilling at this stage to back a venture deep into enemy territory.

By this time, had Lyon been a less determined individual, he might have called it a day. However, as he had no intention of abandoning his plan, he sought, and gained through personal ties with the Victorian Governor, an audience with the Governor

General, Lord Gowrie. Unlike the Americans, who had long since severed their political and emotional ties with the British Empire, Gowrie was able to appreciate the significance of Wavell's letter. By July 17 Lyon was in conference with the Australian Naval Board and Director of Naval Intelligence, Commander R. Long. Having just been appointed to help set up a brand new, clandestine organisation known as the Allied Intelligence Bureau (AIB), Long embraced Lyon's plan with enthusiasm.

At about the same time that Lyon had arrived in Fremantle, AIB, the instrument by which Long and the Navy would make Jaywick a reality, was being evolved. Financed by American, British, Australian and Dutch Governments, its brief was to first amalgamate and then expand all existing intelligence agencies, including Britain's Special Operations Executive (SOE), of which Lyon, Campbell, Morris and Mott were already a part. Designed to cover a broad spectrum, AIB was split into four sections — the RAN's long established 'Coastwatching' organisation (now renamed North Eastern Area or NEA), whose agents relayed shipping and aircraft movements from the islands to the north; a specialised propaganda unit known as Far East Liaison Office (FELO); a secret intelligence agency (SIA), and finally, Mott's baby, the bland-sounding Inter-Allied Services Department (ISD) which was basically the Australian equivalent of SOE.

Some weeks before Lyon's arrival, ISD had begun operating from headquarters set up in a mansion in the Melbourne suburb of South Yarra. With Mott already on side, Commander Long found no problem in having Mott and his colleague, Major Trappes-Lomax, agree that Jaywick should be a joint Navy/SOE effort. It was decided that the Navy would provide guidance and assistance but in all other respects Jaywick would be controlled and funded by SOE in London, which had already sent a substantial amount of money for that purpose. With these administrative problems ironed out, cash waiting in the bank and *Krait* expected to arrive at any time, Lyon began to plan Operation Jaywick in earnest.

A few days later, news was received from India that engine trouble had delayed *Krait*'s departure date and that the ship could not be expected before August 4. With the expedition not scheduled to leave Australia until early December this information did not unduly concern Lyon, whose priorities at this stage lay in finding an able 2IC (second-in-command) for the operation.

He finally selected Donald Davidson, an immensely capable, very fit individual of boundless energy and enthusiasm. English-born, Davidson had spent a number of years working firstly as a jackeroo in outback Australia and then for a timber company in the jungles of the Far East, before accepting a commission with the Royal Naval Volunteer Reserve in Singapore.

Once roped into Lyon's mission, Lieutenant Davidson wasted no time rounding up the necessary volunteers. On August 6, within days of being rescued from the boring desk job he had been given after his evacuation from Singapore, he had presented himself at Melbourne's Flinders Naval Depot and selected eighteen young sailors. The fifteen who ultimately survived Davidson's lengthy and gruelling physical selection trials at a training camp near Melbourne were given a week's leave and ordered to report to the Naval Base at Sydney's Garden Island at noon on September 6. From here they would be transported to a secret training establishment known only as Camp X.

Such was Davidson's efficiency in organising his volunteers that Training Camp X, chosen by Lyon because of its remote location high on a cliff face overlooking the Hawkesbury River estuary, was barely ready in time. Carved out of virgin bush by the sweated labour of Davidson and Morris, who had arrived in Australia with Campbell on July 30, the camp consisted of about a dozen tents more or less lined up before a whitewashed flagpole. The tents lay between a small stream and a rocky outcrop to the rear of the camp. Morris, after recovering from the initial shock of two reptilian eyes staring at him from beneath his stretcher, soon became accustomed to the slithering sound of snakes as they passed through his tent en route to their usual watering hole.

But the snakes were only a minor inconvenience. The site, with sweeping views across the Hawkesbury, was magnificent. More importantly, being situated on an arm of the river (Refuge Bay) and accessible only by foot through the bush or after a steep and difficult climb from the water, the camp was unlikely to have any unexpected visitors.

Given a very free rein and aided by bundles of seemingly unlimited cash which flowed from the coffers of SOE to Jaywick's administrative office in an undercover flat at 15 Onslow Gardens, Potts Point, Sydney, Lyon had no trouble in obtaining the equipment and personnel needed for the training programme.

Davidson, who was responsible for this side of the operation, had designed a curriculum that was definitely not for the fainthearted. As soon as his recruits arrived at the camp they were subjected to an almost round-the-clock programme of most taxing exercises. It was tough going at first but Davidson's methods were such that after a few weeks he was able to report that not only were his men exceptionally fit, but they were also becoming expert in the art of folboat paddling, unarmed combat, explosives and guerilla warfare tactics.

It was just as well that Davidson did not actually require *Krait*'s presence for training purposes. By September 6, the date on which the training programme began, the vessel was well and truly overdue. When the expected date of arrival, August 4, had come and gone with no sign of the ship, Campbell had dispatched a signal seeking information and reminding India that Jaywick's latest departure date was December 1. With no satisfactory reply forthcoming, a flurry of signals had then been transmitted, asking whether Reynolds could make up for lost time by being in Broome, West Australia by the beginning of November at the latest. The answer that Reynolds hoped to have *Krait* there at the end of September was evidently not particularly reassuring, for a further signal was sent on September 7 seeking details of the route, a definite arrival date and confirmation that the ship *had* actually sailed.

Any relief provided by the answers to these queries was shortlived. On October 3, India signalled that major engine trouble had so disrupted the timetable that assistance was now being sought to ship both Reynolds and the *Krait* to Sydney on the first available vessel.

Alone in India, Reynolds was almost beside himself with frustration. The routine engine service in Madras had turned into a real headache when it was revealed that besides an additional major overhaul, *Krait* needed her main bearings and big ends re-metalled, her inlet port re-welded and her circulating pump repaired. As Reynolds was informed that this work could only be carried out by specialists at the South Indian Railway Workshops, he had sailed to Mandapam in October, where he handed the ship over to the Marine Superintendant — one Lieutenant-Commander Seaton, a former submarine engineer. However, Reynolds's troubles were still far from over. The clutch now required attention. Since this work could not be carried out in Mandapam, he took the ship to Bombay, where a new squad of mechanics, this time from the Royal Indian Naval Dockyard, took over. Perhaps the only advantage gained by this detour was that in Bombay Reynolds was able to obtain a replacement for the faulty air compressor and the auxiliary motor. By the greatest good fortune, a company known as Greaves Cotton had two brand new, English-made Ruston Hornsby motors, with which it was persuaded to part.

Back in Australia, Jock Campbell was so alarmed by the constant delays that on October 29 he urged Commander Long to scrap all plans to use *Krait* for the operation. His suggestion to use Seine-net trawlers or pearling luggers instead may have gained approval had not India signalled that *Krait* was on board the P&O Company's steamer *Shillong Shillong* and would be in a state of readiness on arrival. However, elation that the ship was at last on her way was soon shattered when it was learned that *Shillong Shillong*'s sailing date had been put back another two weeks. Concerned that any more hold-ups would throw the whole operation completely out of whack, a now despairing Campbell sought and received confirmation that *Krait* would be in an operational condition as soon as she was unloaded. The next day, however, India retracted this guarantee, leaving Lyon and Campbell with no alternative but to hope that Reynolds would somehow manage to have all repairs completed while the ship was in transit. It was not until November 24 that *Shillong Shillong* finally left Bombay.

When the ship berthed in Sydney early on Christmas Day, there was no reception committee. The super fit, highly efficient Jaywick team had been given four days' leave and the dockyards were idle — the festive season taking priority over the fact that there was a war in progress. By the time the holidaying labour force returned to arrange *Krait*'s removal from the steamer's deck, it was January 4. For the next eight days, the RAN engineers made up for lost time, repairing damage that had occurred to the hull during transit and refitting the interior to accommodate a mass of stores and equipment.

Although any hope of carrying out the raid on a revised date of 15 February 1943, the first anniversary of the fall of Singapore, had long since been abandoned, Davidson did not let up on his training programme. If anything, it intensified, with maintenance of morale just as important as keeping up fitness, particularly when it was learned on January 13 that *Krait*, having finally been victualled and cleared to leave Sydney Harbour, had been stopped by a cracked cylinder head. Delayed even further by poor engine timing, it was not until four days later, at 9.15 on the morning of January 17, that the ship rounded Challenger Head and dropped anchor in Refuge Bay.

The reception was tumultuous. Bursts of machine-gun fire reverberated around the sandstone cliffs, drowning out raucous shouts of welcome. Unable to contain their impatience, two members of the team went out to meet her in HMAS *Lyon* — a small, two-man, plywood kayak which Davidson and one of the trainees had built. When the excitement had been reduced to a manageable level, Morris and the rest of the men spent the remainder of the day transferring folboats and gear to the already cramped holds of the ship and stowing miscellaneous items in every available nook and cranny.

At six o'clock the following morning, after farewelling Campbell who, with the help of two of the four recruits not selected for the mission, was to finalise the dismantling of Camp X, they weighed anchor and *Krait* was finally on her way. On board were Reynolds, Lyon, Davidson, Morris, Morris's cat Cleopatra, Leading Telegraphist Donald Sharples, Hobbs the cook, Stoker Manson and the two officers and eight men who had finally been chosen for the operation. When a leading seaman joined the ship in Brisbane, the expedition would number nineteen. (See Appendix III.)

It was a tight squeeze. With eighteen men, stores for six months, fuel, weapons, explosives, equipment and radio gear, space was at a premium, so much so that there was no proper life-boat — the dinghy *Supply*, left behind at Garden Island, having

H.M.A.S KRAIT
DECK PLAN AFT

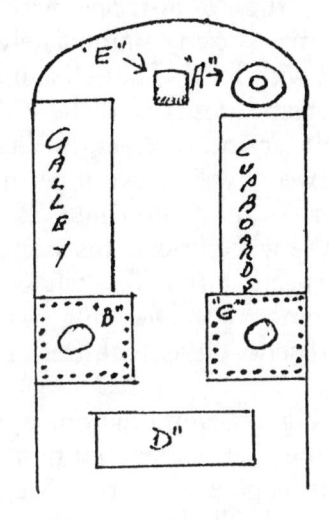

"A" = HEADS
"B" = WATER TANK 266 GALLS
"C" = " " 136 "
"D" = GRAVITY TANK TO ENGINE.
"E" SAMPSON POST.

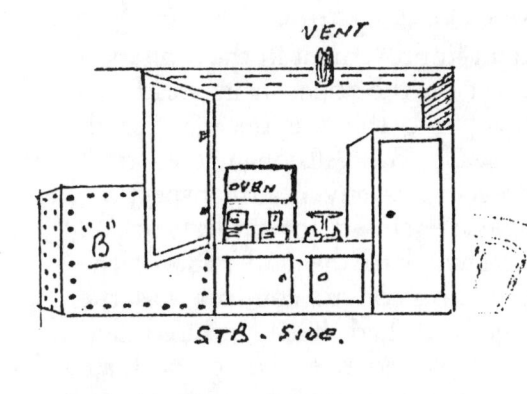

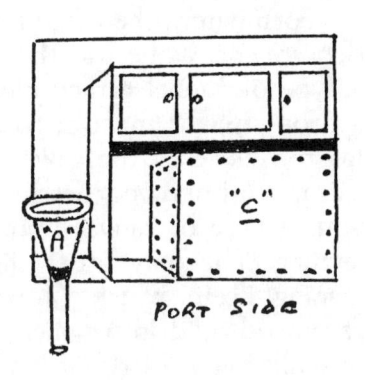

GALLEY
2 LANES BLUE THERMACS AND OVEN.
PLUS PRIMUS STOVE.
TOP OF GRAVITY TANK WAS MESS TABLE.

Sketch plan of *Krait*'s domestic arrangements, by Sid O'Dwyer, a crew member on the vessel, 1944-5.

been replaced by two rafts. The hold closest to the engine room was filled with diesel fuel, the for'ard one with limpets and explosives, while hold number two, immediately behind the foremost hold, was stacked with food. The remaining hold, fitted with a steep wooden ladder and designated the 'Officers' Mess', contained a wireless transmitter and receiver, medical equipment, batteries, three bunks — two of which were permanently laden with equipment and stores — and everything else that did not have a home. The roof of the wheelhouse was stacked with items of miscellany, concealed beneath tarpaulins, while a great chunk of the space on the engine-room housing was utilised to accommodate drums of kerosene, diesel fuel, fresh foodstuffs and a weapons box.

Not surprisingly, sleeping accommodation, apart from the cleared bunk in the mess, the chart-table-cum-bunk arrangement in the wheelhouse and the engineer's berth, was non-existent. With all available space on deck filled with water tanks and more fuel drums, those not on watch or engaged in other duties were forced to snatch their sleep on the small area left free on the engine-room housing or in hammocks slung across it.

Fortunately, there had been an improvement in the sanitation department. Gone was the bucket on the rope. In its stead was a type of funnel arrangement, set into the rear deck and with a drop straight through to the sea below. Although it was still far too close to the galley to ever pass any health inspection, this much-improved 'head' had been enclosed, for modesty's sake, with a type of canvas booth, fastened to the underside of the awning. The only other slight concession to comfort was the awning itself, which Morris noticed had been repaired and revamped, and into which two flaps had been cut to facilitate watchkeeping. Made of sturdy marine ply covered with strong, khaki-coloured bituminised paper, and with faded canvas side-blinds of a similar shade that could be rolled up or down, it stretched from the wheelhouse to the stern, providing good shelter from the elements and a screen from prying eyes.

Despite the cramped conditions and an increasing swell, the voyage north could have been bearable had *Krait* not been plagued with mechanical problems. Five hours out of Refuge Bay the Deutz engine suddenly died. After bleeding the fuel lines of great

A Plan Unfolds

amounts of air and water, Reynolds coaxed it back to life, only to have it break down again almost immediately, stopped this time by an overheated clutch.

To the chagrin of all on board, Reynolds hoisted the sail, turned the ship before the wind and radioed for assistance. Help was not long in coming. Anxious to avoid *Krait*'s being blown out of the water by overzealous shore batteries or naval patrol craft, Naval Intelligence had circulated a detailed description of the ship and alerted all depots between Sydney and Darwin to be on the lookout for her. As an added precaution, to preclude any possibility of mistaken identity, '*Kofuku Maru 2283*' had been removed from the bow and the name '*Krait*' painted in large block capitals on two wooden planks that were attached to the wheelhouse roof.

Not wishing to appear more ridiculous than absolutely necessary when HMAS *Peterson* arrived from Newcastle to answer *Krait*'s call for help, Reynolds had the crew lower the sail before the minesweeper appeared, only to lose what small headway he had. Unable to manoeuvre, *Krait* collided with the larger vessel, damaging her bows. After considerable trouble a line was secured and the ship was taken in tow, only to have the kingpost, which was riddled with dry rot, part company with the deck. While *Krait* suffered the further indignity of being towed by the stern, Reynolds continued to struggle with the clutch. About three kilometres from Newcastle, and just in time to save them from the humiliation of being towed into port, the engine spluttered back into life.

Determined to make a better impression on their arrival in Newcastle, Reynolds took a flying leap onto the wharf, stern rope in hand, as the ship docked. Unfortunately, his forward propulsion was stopped mid-flight when the rope fouled, jerking him up short and spearheading him into the harbour, a good three metres from the wharf. When he spluttered to the surface, still clutching the rope and plastered with oil, and discovered that his glasses — his one and only pair — had been consigned to the deep, the entire dockyard cowered under the torrent of his abuse. When the ship was finally repaired his disposition was not improved in the slightest by the news that further passage was prohibited for at least two days, owing to reports of Japanese submarine activity off the coast.

Perhaps the only bright side to the interminable delays was the size of Reynolds's remuneration. Not bound by any financial constraint, ISD evidently had a completely free hand when it came to negotiating rates of pay for civilians attached to Lyon's outfit. Reynolds's wage was set at a massive seventy-five pounds a month — about two and a half times the going rate.

By the time they reached Brisbane, Reynolds figured he had earned his money. The voyage of 'The Reluctant Dragon', as Lyon had dubbed *Krait*, was proving to be a real headache. Stuttering up the New South Wales coast, she had been laid low by complaints as diverse as choked bilge pumps, a faulty generator, a seized front-end bearing, blocked lubricating pipes and a seized air compressor. As if the mechanical faults had not been enough, the ship had then run into heavy seas. To make matters worse, the men's morale, lowered by constant bouts of seasickness, plummetted even further when Morris's feline companion, Cleopatra, was washed overboard and drowned.

It was a seedy looking bunch and a waterlogged ship that eventually put into Brisbane at the end of January. While the rest headed for the beach at Surfers Paradise to improve their tans and indulge in a spot of rest, recreation and exercise, Lyon and Reynolds stayed in town. Reynolds gave his full attention to *Krait*, leaving Lyon to concentrate on the finer details such as the supply of pseudo-Malay sarongs from the Brisbane firm of Overell's Ltd (a company owned by the family of Jaywick's explosive expert, Sub-Lieutenant Bert Overell), and to catch up on the latest intelligence.

On February 6, Jock Campbell arrived from Sydney with a volunteer civilian engineer, one H. Hazewinkel, who confirmed Reynolds's gravest fears. Before *Krait* could continue any further a complete engine overhaul would be necessary. He informed Reynolds and Campbell that, although he had stockpiled in Sydney a selection of spare parts (fortuitously removed by Lever Brothers from their trading posts in the South Pacific before the Japanese took up residence), many others would have to be especially made. The delay, he figured, would be about a month.

While the engineers swarmed over the ship, and Campbell occupied himself by compiling a comprehensive record of her many mechanical defects, others were equally as busy. By the time the rest of the team, now very fit and very tanned, arrived back in Brisbane after a short leave, they discovered that the two small petrol stoves in the galley had been replaced by a safer, more efficient model and the entire foredeck had been coated with a bullet-proof marine glue compound. When the ship left for Townsville on March 2 they also realised that Stoker Manson had gone and that there were now two new crewmen in residence.

The first of the newcomers, Leading Seaman Kevin Cain, commonly known as 'Cobber', was in many ways similar to Bill Reynolds. The strong silent type who went about his business with the minimum of fuss, Cobber Cain was an experienced and practical seaman who said little, noticed much, enjoyed a quiet life and, if absolutely necessary, was quite prepared to resort to fisticuffs to achieve it. However, it was only on rare occasions that the normally even-tempered and universally liked Cain had to flex his muscles. One black look from this handsome, dark-haired sailor, who had a distinct advantage over most in that he was built like a professional wrestler, was more than sufficient to reduce the most fractious individual to a state of total acquiescence.

Krait's poor mechanical showing on the voyage up from Sydney had been the reason for Stoker Manson's sudden disappearance. Although Lyon conceded that he had been an 'able and attentive watchkeeper', he had not the slightest idea on how to carry out the most basic repairs, making him a dead loss in the engineering department. Concerned by Manson's lack of mechanical expertise, Lyon had replaced him with an engineer named Paddy McDowell, a really tough old salt with an unsurpassed passion for engines and well versed in the art of ocean-going subterfuge. A sailor in the Royal Navy during the First World War, Paddy had served on Q ships — the code name for merchantmen used as decoys against enemy submarines. Loaded with timber to prevent their sinking too quickly if holed by torpedoes or shells, the ships, mostly tramp steamers and colliers, had looked defenceless enough — so defenceless, Paddy told his young shipmates, that submarines were often tricked into surfacing. It was not until the freighters opened up with guns cunningly concealed behind collapsible structures that the submariners, completely vulnerable upon the surface, realised their error.

Although Paddy had no idea of what *Krait* was really up to, it was obvious, from the long-range fuel tanks, the vast amount of supplies and the arsenal stored below decks, that this was no pleasure cruise. Either way, it did not matter to him. Interested in only one thing, Paddy rarely emerged from below decks, so besotted was he by his oily, smelly engine, on which he lavished the utmost care and attention.

The ship was off Fraser Island, about one-third of the way to Townsville, when trouble again reared its head. Almost simultaneously, an oil pipe burst and Donald Davidson went down with malaria. While the patient was taken to hospital, mechanics were dispatched from Maryborough to assist Paddy with the necessary repairs.

The engine was being warmed up for a trial run when Morris, who was on the foredeck, was startled to hear a violent explosion, not unlike that of a hand grenade. While most of the crew sensibly abandoned ship, Morris hurried aft. Peering through an engine room skylight he saw that a piston had speared through the engine casing, setting off a chain reaction. As the connecting rod had wrapped itself around the cam shaft, spewing chunks of metal around the engine room, all those in close proximity, apart from Paddy, had decided that the best place to be was definitely over the side. When the excitement had died down, Paddy McDowell sadly inspected the damage. His engine was beyond salvation. In this last mad frenzy it had completely self-destructed.

Perhaps it was a combination of the engine's sudden and spectacular demise and the indignity of being towed into Townsville that now caused Reynolds to lose his temper with one of the crew. Evidently provoked beyond endurance, Reynolds had ended the argument by literally decking the source of his discontent. Although he was to prepare a case for some kind of enquiry into his behaviour for 'striking a seaman' and using 'unseaman like methods of coercion', Reynolds was never brought to book. In an ironic twist of fate, it was probably the hopeless state of *Krait*'s engine, as much as his civilian status, that kept him out of the court room.

A Plan Unfolds

On March 27, a fortnight after *Krait* arrived in Townsville, it was decided that unless another engine could be found, Jaywick would have to be indefinitely postponed. With no prospect of a suitable marine engine materialising in the near future, the stores and useless engine were removed. Since there was no engine or gear to act as ballast, the empty ship was towed with a great deal of trouble to Cairns, where all but the operatives were dispersed. Reynolds, being a civilian, was now footloose, fancy-free and out of a job.

He returned to his family in Melbourne, determined, one way or another, to get back into the war. His refusal to accept a Royal Naval commission in India, on the grounds that the rank of temporary lieutenant would have made him subordinate to his son, Bill Reynolds jnr, was now a mixed blessing. Although on the one hand he had sidestepped official censure over the incident with the crew member, Reynolds had to face the fact that he was now an ordinary citizen, and a very middle-aged one at that. But, like Ivan Lyon, Reynolds was not about to give up. Exploiting all his existing contacts to the full he managed, over the next few months, to convince AIB, and the Americans in particular, that he was indispensible to the war effort. After a series of protracted meetings and persuasive argument, Reynolds overcame all obstacles and became part of a highly secret Allied spy network, whose real aim was known only to a few. An exceedingly irregular outfit, operating under the cover name of 'United States Bureau of Economic Warfare', it specialised in recruiting people who had expert local knowledge to operate behind enemy lines in the Far East.

Although the risks were high, so too was the monetary reward. It was an elated Reynolds who, after months of negotiation, astounded his wife by tipping onto the matrimonial bed a pile of US currency with the announcement 'there will be plenty more where this came from'. However, in spite of this change in fortune and his irrepressible enthusiasm, Reynolds was also a realist. Aware that, as he officially did not exist, all financial assistance would cease should he fail to return from one of his missions, he decided to take steps to ensure his family's future financial security. Without telling anyone what he was up to, he took the advice of his solicitors and lodged a claim with the Colonial Office for salvage rights to *Krait*.

Unaware that legal proceedings would soon be in progress to claim compensation for a ship to which neither they, nor their organisation, had any right, Lyon and Campbell combed Australia for a replacement engine. It was fortunate that a reorganisation of AIB, which had taken place in February that year, gave them almost unlimited powers.

ISD had vanished, along with its Director, Edgerton Mott, who had become frustrated by interference from the Controller of AIB. In place of ISD was Special Operations Australia (SOA), known to all but the top echelons by the innocuous sounding Services Reconnaissance Department or SRD. So tight was SRD's security that its real name was used only at the highest levels, and then only when absolutely necessary. Answerable to Australia's Commander-in-Chief, General Sir Thomas Blamey, and with direct access to General Douglas MacArthur, Supreme Allied Commander, it purported for various reasons to still be a part of AIB. In reality and in common with the propaganda unit FELO, it was no longer under AIB's direct control — a fact known only to its most senior personnel.

So keen was General Blamey to keep SRD sacrosanct that he scotched plans to dispense with an administrative body known as Z Special Unit. Set up in June 1942 as a holding unit for the large number of Australian Army personnel who had been transferred to special operations, it owed its name to a military wireless establishment known as Z Experimental Station, whose facilities it had taken over in Cairns. As Z Unit had been competently handling such mundane chores as transportation, accommodation, pay, stores and equipment, Blamey decided it was too handy to lose. Since SRD was now virtually independent, another administrative arm was formed in April 1943 to service AIB, which controlled several units including the Coastwatchers. For no obviously apparent reason, the new outfit was dubbed 'M Special Unit'.

With a carte blanche as far as acquisition of stores was concerned, it is little wonder that Lyon, through SRD, was able to home in on a suitable engine for *Krait* — a 103-horsepower, six-cylinder Gardner diesel. Unfortunately, it was in Tasmania,

A Plan Unfolds

about as far away from Cairns as it was possible to be. Worse, having just taken delivery of a commodity that was in exceedingly short supply, Gardner's Tasmanian agents, A. G. Webster and Sons, were not simply about to hand it over. However, such was the power of SRD that the engine, previously earmarked for army use, was diverted to Jaywick.

If Lyon was elated by this news, he was ecstatic after consultations with Gardner's expert in Victoria, Mr Bert Bevan-Davies. Bert, who later described the Gordon Highlander as 'a man among men and the most charismatic man I have ever met', convinced Lyon that the Gardner was more than capable of doing whatever it was that Lyon required of it. Told only that the marine diesel engine was needed for a special mission that might require it to run non-stop for a month. Bert spent hours with Lyon, handling spare parts, matching them to specification manuals and visiting marine establishments to see similar engines working, until Lyon was as conversant with the machinery as any mechanic.

Bert found Lyon's capacity to absorb vast amounts of information almost as astounding as his scrupulous attention to detail. So determined was Lyon to ensure that should *Krait* fall into enemy hands she would not betray her origins, he and Bert stayed up night after night until the wee small hours personally removing every trace of the Gardner name, not only from the engine but from every single spare part. When the job was completed, Lyon, mindful that Bert had given unstintingly of his time and energy to a mission about which he had to remain completely ignorant, shook hands and said 'If all goes well you will know what you helped prepare. If not, you will never know.'

As soon as 2250 pounds sterling had been handed over as payment to the Hobart importer, the now anonymous engine, with its mountain of spare parts, was loaded onto a ship and dispatched to the far north. After months of uncertainty, Lyon allowed himself the luxury of breathing a little more easily. Operation Jaywick was at last under way — almost.

CHAPTER SIX

Into Enemy Waters

In mid-June, even as the engine was being crated for its voyage to Cairns, the powers-that-be at Allied Headquarters were having second thoughts. After twelve months of very expensive planning, preparation and training, they decided that to attack an enemy port in the way Lyon intended was impossible. Lyon was informed that unless someone could come up with something fast, Jaywick would have to be abandoned. Just when it seemed all would be lost, one of Lyon's SRD colleagues, Captain Sam Carey, came to the rescue. In the manner befitting a member of a commando organisation, Carey pulled a stunt that proved beyond all doubt that such a raid was not only feasible, but had every chance of success.

With his own plan to carry out a limpet attack on enemy vessels in Rabaul Harbour cancelled in May, owing to a lack of ready transport, and knowing that Jaywick's fate hung in the balance, Carey decided to mount a dummy raid on Allied shipping in the Queensland port of Townsville. Such was the brilliant execution of the operation, carried out on the night of June 19, that his men not only penetrated the harbour defences undetected; they also managed to attach mock limpet-mines to fifteen ships. When the limpets, which were thought to be genuine, were sighted the next day the panic was colossal. So was the uproar when it was discovered that Carey was the culprit. But it was worth it. On June 20, courtesy of Sam Carey, Operation Jaywick was given the final seal of approval.

Five weeks later when Paddy McDowell went down to the wharf at Cairns to collect the new engine, he discovered that although the engine was intact, all the tools, as he so succinctly put it, were 'well ratted'. Evidently the sight of such hard-to-come-by supplies, clearly visible through the damaged sides of the packing crate, had proved too great a temptation for roaming scavengers, who had swooped. However, Paddy obviously had good contacts, for the problem of the missing tools was solved and the engine transported to Smith Creek, a tributary of the Barron River, where *Krait* was waiting to be transformed from hulk to ocean-going vessel. As soon as shipwrights and engineers, sent up especially from Walker's shipyard in Maryborough, had built up and strengthened the bed plate to ensure that the shaft alignment was correct, the new engine was lowered into place and installed.

With the schedule tight, the new engine-room housing was a poor apology for the original, which had been removed, along with the defunct engine, at Townsville. In place of the sturdy construction with its glass side-panels set into detailed joinery was a nondescript timber affair into whose roof had been cut two hatches, propped open by a pair of battens. This and the wheelhouse had then been painted an indeterminate shade of brown which, if nothing else, more or less matched the equally drab checkered curtains hanging at the wheelhouse's grimy windows. The only obvious advantage with the new engine-housing design was that by dropping the hatches the engine room could be quickly blacked out at night — a feature that had its disadvantage in that the air-flow was reduced to zero, making the below deck area not only stuffy but unbearably hot.

The cramped conditions and the sauna-like heat had no effect on Paddy, who was so busy he didn't have time to notice anything. With the engine installed to his exacting specifications, it was off to the slips, where a new propeller was fitted. Then, and only then, was Paddy ready for a test run. Fully aware that the future of the operation depended upon how well he and his offsiders had done their job, it was with a sense of excitement as well as apprehension, that he put *Krait* into the water and started her up.

Never was a ship's engineer more ecstatic. Compared to the Deutz, which Paddy now derisively declared had sounded like 'a brass band in a railway cutting', the Gardner literally purred. Paddy McDowell was in seventh heaven.

So too was Ivan Lyon. While Paddy had been busy organising the installation of the engine, Davidson had rounded up the team, most of whom were at the nearby Z Experimental Station, leaving Lyon to concentrate on fine-tuning the operational plans.

It was a confident party leader who now scrutinised the details, convinced that his luck had changed for the better. Dogged by disaster and disappointment for so long, he was now inundated with good news. Jaywick was back on the rails; he, Morris and Reynolds had been decorated by the King for their rescue work in Sumatra; and, miracles of miracles, he had received word about his wife Gabrielle and small son Clive, whom he had last seen in Singapore in December 1941 prior to their evacuation to Australia. Told in May that they had been lost at sea while attempting to join him in India, Ivan now learned that Gabrielle and Clive were not dead but were alive and well, albeit in a civilian internment camp in Japan. It was an understandably elated Ivan Lyon, MBE, who now gave his full and undivided attention to Operation Jaywick.

Lyon, who had now been promoted to the rank of major, perused operational plans that had been substantially altered. While the installation of the long-range Gardner engine meant that they would no longer have to call at Darwin for fuel and Hope Island (where a supply dump was to have been set up), he realised that the decision to scrap the incendiary attack on land installations was a mixed blessing. Although the operation was greatly simplified, and the attack team reduced to a more manageable three officers and three men, with two reservists, the reshuffle had resulted in the loss of explosives expert Bert Overell and another very able officer, Captain 'Gort' Chester, making the raiding party, consisting of Lyon, Davidson and five men, an officer short. Also needed were a new navigator, telegraphist and cook to replace Reynolds, Sharples and Hobbs, whose duties or inclinations had taken them elsewhere.

Since daredevil and experienced mariners with extensive knowledge of South-East Asian waters, as well as navigational expertise, were a rare species, a replacement for Reynolds was by far Lyon's most pressing problem. Realising that no one would ever come up to the calibre of Reynolds, for whom he had great affection and deep admiration, Lyon was compelled to lower his sights. After scouring SRD's ranks he settled on Sub-Lieutenant Edward Carse — a middle-aged RAN reservist with an unfortunate affinity for alcohol — whose impulsive decision to join SRD had been precipitated by a spat with his wife. Accepted into the organisation primarily because of his experience on luggers operating in the seas to the north of Australia, Carse was beginning to regret his hasty decision. The exciting career he had expected to find in North Queensland with special operations had been a real disappointment. His job of trying to turn Indonesian recruits into seamen was less than riveting and his so-called training vessel, a run-down launch named *Gnair* (which had been abandoned in Cairns after successfully evacuating a small party from Japanese-occupied Rabaul), was even more dilapidated looking than *Krait*. Consequently, when Lyon offered him the position as navigator for Operation Jaywick, Carse, who had sworn that he would never again volunteer for anything, accepted.

Neither his appearance nor his demeanor impressed Taffy Morris, who was used to associating with officers who not only looked but who also acted the part. According to Morris, Carse — with his less than immaculate uniform, his generally down-at-heel air, and with the effect of a lifetime of intemperate drinking habits clearly etched upon his weatherworn face — would have been more at home on a tramp steamer. However, Morris's opinion carried no weight. Lyon, who was in no position to look a gift horse in the mouth, had already signed him on.

Within days Lyon had also recruited one of the two remaining non-operative crew members. Leading Telegraphist Young, RANR, a wireless fanatic from West Australia, replaced Sharples who, apart from being dissatisfied with his appointment to *Krait*, for which his temperament was ill-suited, had now married and was hence reluctant to proceed. His substitute, also married but definitely not reluctant — the youthful looking, rather pale-faced Young — was as single-minded about his wireless transceiver as Paddy McDowell was about his engine.

Surprisingly, finding a new cook was not as simple as it sounded. When Lyon and Campbell had learned that ginger-haired Allan 'Bluey' Hobbs was no longer available they had searched without success for an Asian cook, whose presence on deck might help convince an enemy plane that *Krait* was simply a Japanese fishing boat going about her normal business. With Asiatics either unable or unwilling to take up the offer and time running out, they frantically canvassed for a cook — any cook. It was not until the eleventh hour that Lyon found a volunteer — a small, curly-haired corporal who was awaiting discharge from the Australian Army on medical grounds.

That a cook and not an engineer was required was no deterrent to Scots-born Andrew Crilley. Conveniently forgetting that he was supposed to be invalided out of the army and ignoring the fact that his expertise lay elsewhere, he managed to convince Lyon that he was the man for the job. As Crilley was keen, unmarried and said he could cook, Lyon quickly agreed to have him.

He joined the mission's only other member of the AIF — a recently recruited lieutenant by the name of Robert Page. Well educated and immensely good-natured, this dark-haired officer, whose handsome looks would not have been out of place on the silver screen, was instantly welcomed on board. Having partially trained as a doctor, and being one of the madcap bunch who had raided Townsville shipping, Bob Page was an especially valuable addition to the Jaywick team.

At one minute to midnight on August 4, a mere nine days after Paddy had collected the engine from the Cairns waterfront, *Krait* was ready to sail to Townsville to retrieve the stores that had been off-loaded there the previous March. As the navigational instruments had not yet arrived, navigation during the thirty-hour voyage south was very much a matter of point-to-point coasting. While the ship was in Townsville being victualled, the instruments, with the exception of the Azimuth Mirror (used to take precise compass bearings) arrived, allowing them to make much better time on the return voyage to Cairns. After spending a full day tarring the ropes and sail, purchasing a dinghy, taking on board a spare propeller and making some mechanical adjustments, they left port at 8.30 pm on August 9, bound for Thursday Island — a small settlement lying just off the tip of Queensland's Cape York Peninsula.

On the face of it, *Krait*, alias *Kofuku Maru* and *Suey Sin Fah*, carried a most incongruous crew. First and foremost of the fourteen-man party was Englishman Ivan Lyon, commanding officer, fearless soldier and experienced amateur sailor; his deputy Donald Davidson, a one-time jackeroo and teak forester who, as he himself cheerfully admitted, had gone to the Naval Base in Singapore in 1941 to play a game of dice and had come out with a naval commission; Ted Carse, the substitute navigator, whose resolve, after a lifetime of alcoholic dependency, had yet to be tested; dashing Bob Page, a third-year medical student whose idealism had prompted him to give up his studies and volunteer for special operations; Taffy Morris, Lyon's devoted medical orderly who, like all Welshmen, had the extraordinary capacity to sing even when the chips were down; strong, silent Cobber Cain, a no-nonsense type sailor who was eminently practical in the ways of the sea; Andy Crilley, an 'invalid' army engineer who had yet to prove his culinary skills; the introspective telegraphist Horrie Young, whose quiet manner belied his ability to belong to such an outfit; Irish-born Scotsman Paddy McDowell, engineer extraordinaire who, having served Great Britain in the First War, was perfectly content to line up for his adopted country in the Second; and last, but by no means least, the five volunteer sailors whom Donald Davidson had recruited twelve months earlier.

Young and enthusiastic by nature, these five volunteers were fit, strong, highly trained and raring to go. Ranging in age from eighteen to twenty-three, the list was headed by dairy farmer Wally Falls who, being the eldest, was known as Poppa. Amazingly strong, Wally, who had been blessed with good looks and a ready smile, had never been known to lose his cool or his temper, making him a great favourite with everyone, particularly Morris. By way of contrast, eighteen-year-old Freddie Marsh was the life and soul of the party — an irrepressible larrikin whose predilection for practical jokes was offset by his amazing prowess in unarmed combat. Called more often than not 'Boof' because of his rather square-shaped head with its mass of blond curls, Fred had made the transition from apprentice cabinet-maker to commando with consummate ease. His complete opposite was his best mate — a lithe, olive-skinned Queenslander named Andrew Huston. Aged nineteen but looking much younger than Marsh, Andrew was known as Happy Huston — an ironic nickname which harked back to his early days of training when

Sketch plans of *Krait*'s wartime configuration, by Sid O'Dwyer, a crew member on the vessel, 1944-5.

he had had an occasional grumble or two. Iron-willed, Huston had been determined to succeed — a doggedness which had been recognised by Davidson, particularly when it was discovered that in order to gain selection, his pupil had to learn to both swim and fight.

Also aged eighteen, dark-haired Mostyn 'Moss' Berryman was as quiet and reserved as Boof was noisy and outgoing. But still waters ran deep and, like Huston, Davidson recognised that Moss had special abilities — namely the talent to get things done with a minimum of fuss. Indeed, such was his quiet efficiency that Davidson had already earmarked him as being suitable officer material. Equally as quiet was the most senior in rank of the five — Arthur Jones, who answered to Joe and whose dark looks and slightly shorter stature gave him the ability to pass, at a distance, as Japanese. Now an able seaman and the only recruit who had sea experience, Joe had an underlying steadiness which the critical Morris found very reassuring.

Without the Azimuth Mirror to check their position, Carse found navigation to Thursday Island difficult, so difficult in fact that as soon as the moon set at night they anchored lest *Krait* impale herself on one of the many coral reefs that littered the area. Even with the moon and lookouts posted he had trouble and on the fourth night out from Cairns ran aground near Chapman Island. Fortunately there was no damage and the ship proceeded the following day to Thursday Island.

After picking up details of his outward journey and a copy of SRD's latest Intelligence Summary, Lyon made arrangements with the RAAF for air cover. Although they would not be entering enemy territory to reach the next landfall at Exmouth Gulf, Western Australia, *Krait* would have to cross the Gulf of Carpentaria, where Japanese bombers and float planes were constantly attacking shipping in the vicinity of Cape Wessel. With memories of others who had tempted fate by sailing from Singapore on that Black Friday in 1942 still fresh in their minds, it was decided that even with the air cover. Friday August 13 had an ominous ring to it and they delayed their departure until the next morning. While they were preparing to get underway, the paper work for Operation Jaywick finally caught up with the action. Fully fifteen months after Wavell had given Lyon the go-ahead, the mission was given official written approval.

As it turned out, the covering aircraft around the coastline of northern Australia were superfluous. They saw no sign of the enemy and the passage would have been uneventful had it not been for two small incidents. The first mishap, later dubbed The Battle of Carpentaria, occurred shortly after breakfast one morning. As Cobber Cain was attempting to clear a jammed Lewis gun the bullet exploded. In the chain reaction that followed, it glanced off a spare magazine and smashed a bottle of tomato sauce to smithereens before burying itself in the roof.

The horrified initial reaction that there had been wholesale massacre dissipated into amusement when it was discovered that almost all the carnage was not spilt from human arteries but was, in fact, lashings of rich, red tomato sauce. When the sauce was scraped away two casualties were discovered: Berryman, whose legs, arms and chest were peppered with shards of glass, and Morris, who had the misfortune to have been standing on the fuel tank keeping watch through the roof flap and was therefore almost on top of the exploding bottle. Although they were most uncomfortable, the glass splinters that littered his body were the least of his problems. Of far greater concern (to all except Page, who now had a unique opportunity to show off his needlework skills) was Morris's ankle, which had been badly lacerated by a piece of flying metal. While Page stitched away with a blunt and vastly oversized needle, the doughty Welshman lay spreadeagled on the engine-room housing, trying to distract his mind from the excruciating pain by interspersing bursts of tuneless whistling with judicious swigs from the medicinal rum bottle, waves washing over the pitching deck all the while.

Morris, who stubbornly refused Lyon's invitation to be put ashore in Darwin, had still not recovered from his ordeal when they almost ran into serious trouble off the coast of Western Australia. Having successfully negotiated Cape Wessel, their problem stemmed not from enemy aircraft but from the reefs that circled Adele Island, and into which Carse inadvertently strayed. Although it was a mystery how he had crossed the reef in the first place without coming to grief, they avoided ultimate disaster when, after a painstaking search, they managed to find the one and only way out, described by Davidson as 'very foul'.

It was during the last section of the trip that two structural modifications were made — Paddy fitted a silencer to the extremely noisy exhaust and the crew chipped off and dumped the thick bullet proof coating. Ordered as a precaution against enemy strafing, it was obvious that, far from saving their lives, the heavy compound might well be the death of all of them. In all but the calmest seas *Krait*, with an enormous additional weight in her bow, was threatening to take them all to Davey Jones's locker. Once liberated from her two tonnes of overburden, the ship rode infinitely better in the water, allowing them to head at full speed for Potshot, the United States Naval Base situated at Exmouth Gulf.

For the four days that *Krait* was tied up alongside the American submarine repair ship *Chanticleer*, the men, as guests of the US Navy, gorged themselves on turkey and cranberry sauce, ice cream and whisky. While they filled in the spare time between gastronomic feasts by painting *Krait*'s deck a flat, camouflaging grey and removing her name from the wheelhouse roof, Davidson unpacked supplies which had been sent from Melbourne. Within minutes of undoing the packages, he was in a towering rage, for, although the parcels containing spare parts for *Krait* (compasses, anti-glare glasses, mail, telescope and binoculars) were welcome, the four new folboats most definitely were not. Davidson was furious to find that although he had sent exact specifications to England, not one of his instructions had been followed. As it was too late to do anything else, he and the raiding party were forced to spend the rest of their time at Exmouth not in recreational pursuits but in on-the-spot modifications simply to make the framework fit together.

With the problems of the folboats eventually ironed out, *Krait* left her final mooring alongside the supply ship SS *Ondina* late on the afternoon of September 1 bound, so the Americans thought, for Fremantle. However, on moving astern, the coupling key of the intermediate propeller shafting broke, bringing the ship to an abrupt halt. The mission might have foundered there and then had not *Chanticleer* unexpectedly and fortuitously returned to port a few hours later. While the rest of the ship's company showered the Jaywick team with hospitality, *Chanticleer*'s mechanics and engineers worked on *Krait* non-stop. At two o'clock the next afternoon, after a marathon effort, they announced that the job was finished. Cautioning Lyon to nurse the ship as the repairs were only temporary at best, they then farewelled *Krait* for the second time, unaware that she was heading not for the safety of Fremantle but for Java's Lombok Strait.

As soon as they had left the protection of Exmouth Gulf, Mother Nature, as if to test the strength of the repairs, whipped up southerly winds and seas so violent that Horrie Young was thrown out of his hammock. Bruised and dazed, he would have been washed overboard had Boof Marsh not grabbed hold of him. As the water swirled round the wheelhouse, Lyon fought desperately to hold the ship against mountainous waves that battered the port side. Waist deep, the sea poured across the deck, threatening to carry away anyone who did not have a firm hold. Even with the deck armour jettisoned the overloaded ship rolled heavily, lunging from one massive wave to the next until it did not seem possible that she could stay afloat.

Just when it appeared that she must surely capsize under the weight of water trapped in her hull, one of the crew grabbed an axe hanging above the lockers and, with immense presence of mind, chopped a hole in the planking. With agonising slowness, as tonnes of water were released, *Krait* righted herself. As the sea abated, so did the anxiety, and within twenty-four hours the swell had dropped dramatically, making it difficult to imagine that any danger had ever existed.

The following day Lyon lifted the lid on Operation Jaywick, breaking the secrecy that had been so rigidly maintained for more than twelve months. If the rest of the crew was surprised that the target was Singapore and not Surabaya, as they had expected, Taffy Morris was astounded. Never in his wildest dreams had he imagined that Lyon would have the audacity to return to Singapore, which, at this stage of the war, was deep in Japanese-held territory. As he and the rest of the crew clustered eagerly around their leader, they listened wide-eyed as he calmly and succinctly outlined the plans formulated so long ago.

Basically, he told them, the entire operation depended on their ability to masquerade as native fishermen operating a Japanese fishing vessel. To achieve this subterfuge, all uniforms would be discarded in favour of the native-style sarongs made by Overells Ltd and their white skin covered with brown body-stain, which had been especially formulated by the cosmetic company Helena Rubenstein. With *Krait* flying a Japanese flag they would enter the target area, where the raiding party would transfer to folboats, carry out the limpet attack and return to meet *Krait* at a pre-arranged rendezvous two weeks later. If they came under surveillance Lyon, Carse and Jones — the only ones dark enough to have any chance of passing as non-European — were to stay on deck while the others took up action stations. It was hoped that they could convince anyone watching that they were the crew of a local coastal vessel engaged in normal fishing activities.

Although most of the men by now had quite good tans, the attempts to convert them from white Anglo-Saxons to honey-brown Malays were hopeless. Not only did the oily stain adhere to everything except the human skin it was supposed to cover, but it stung abominably and streaked unconvincingly if thinned down to a shade anything less than the deepest brown. With blue eyes impossible to disguise and fair hair totally resistant to colour change, despite repeated applications of the dye, the donning of sarongs, for the most part, was academic. As Carse noted in the ship's log, the crew, far from appearing Malay, 'resemble blackamoors. A more desperate looking crowd I have never seen'. However, despite the obvious shortcomings, they gambled that if viewed from a distance the brown bodies, the native garb and the sight of the Japanese ensign would keep inquisitive craft from coming too close.

Consequently, on the morning of September 6 and to the sound of much cheering and general banter from the sarong-clad throng, Lyon ordered Horrie Young to break out on *Krait*'s stern the red and white flag of Japan. Sewn in absolute secrecy in Melbourne by the wife of Harry Manderson, a civilian attached to SRD, the once pristine flag was now unrecognisable, having been reduced to a filthy rag by liberal doses of engine oil and a general scuffing around the deck.

As they neared Lombok Strait the following day, Lyon's security, which was always tight, became absolute. Since floating cigarettes and matches would be a dead give-away, smoking was

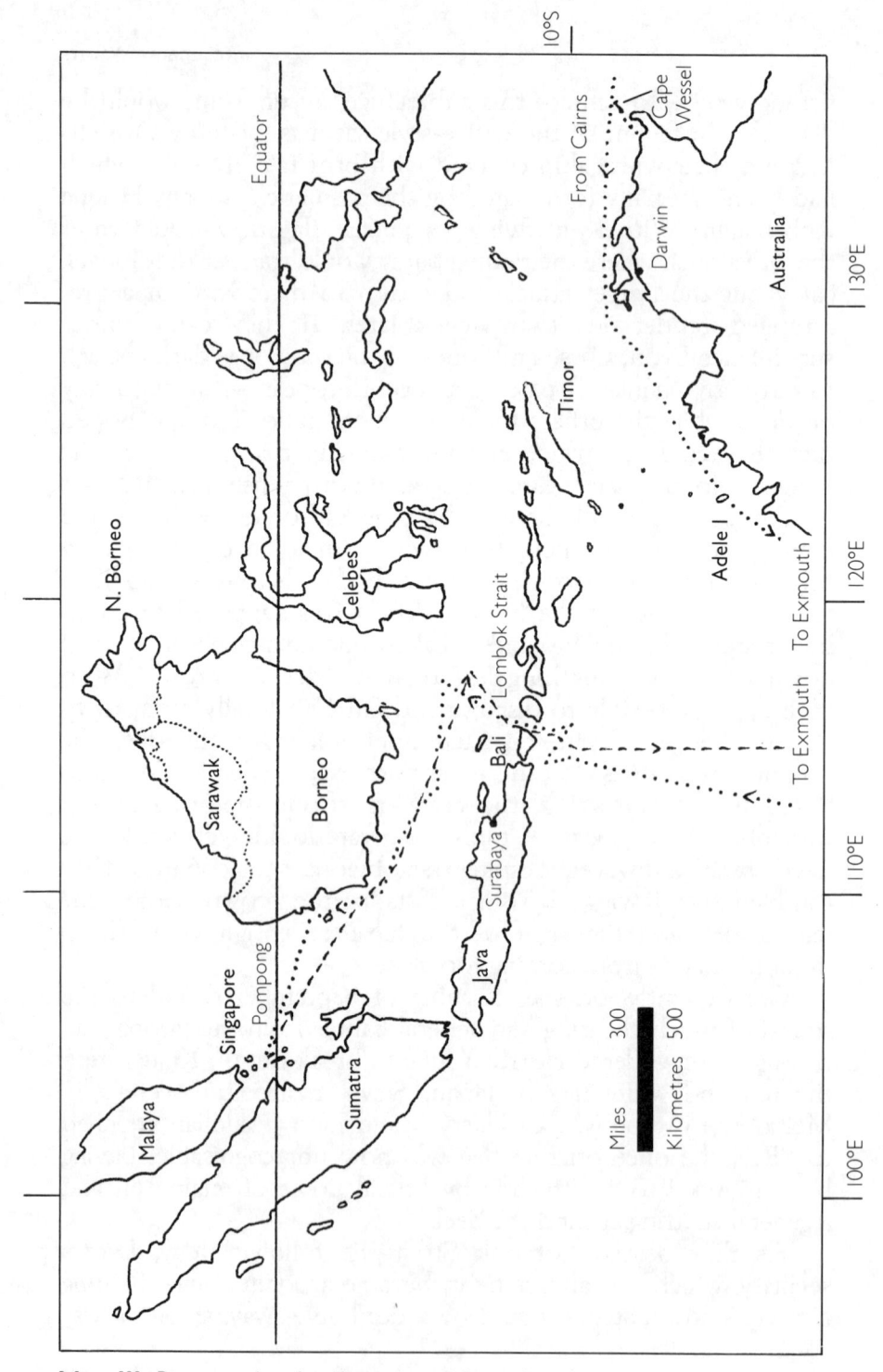

Map III. Routes taken by *Krait* to and from Singapore, for Operation Jaywick.

forbidden, an edict that brought groans of despair from the nicotine-dependent. Also forbidden, somewhat to the consternation of the more fastidious, was the use of toilet paper. Shaving mirrors that might flash in the sunlight were banned above deck by day while a total blackout was in force at night. As an added precaution all refuse had to be placed in sealed tins and sunk by gunfire, lest one skerrick escape and so betray their presence.

Tension was understandably high as the men, now in native disguise, scanned the horizon for the first glimpse of Agung and Rinjani, the towering volcanic peaks that marked the entrance to Lombok Strait. The sight was a long time coming. Despite his mid-afternoon log entry that *Krait* was headed directly for Lombok, Carse was so far off course that at midnight on September 7, hours after they should have been entering the strait, he discovered that they were at the western end of Bali Island instead of to the east. After a radical course alteration he finally located the entrance, twenty-four hours and 270 kilometres later, only to discover that they had missed the tide. With water rushing out of the strait at a fast rate of knots, the error meant that *Krait*, at times, actually went backwards. For almost three hours, while the crew watched the headlights of enemy vehicles on the same stretch of road, the ship made no headway at all. But even when the tide turned, things only marginally improved. Although the pilot book had indicated that visibility would be poor, when daylight came they found that they could see every rock and tree with absolute clarity on the Bali side of the strait. Fortunately, the easterly side, which they had deduced from the presence of a searchlight was probably an enemy base, was shrouded by a slight haze that gave *Krait* some measure of protection. Consequently, it was more good luck than anything else that enabled Carse, at ten o'clock on the morning of September 9, to write in the log 'Thank Christ. We are through the strait'.

Once clear of Lombok *Krait* made good progress. The journey, as she skirted the Kangean Islands en route to the Carimata Straits, south of Borneo, was now so uneventful that Lyon reported it was 'most dull' — an opinion shared by Bob Page, who sought to relieve his boredom by doling out various pills and vitamins to see what effect they would have on his captive human guinea pigs. With the exception of Carse, whose eyes were giving him trouble from the glare, and Morris, whose wound had not healed, they all kept fit and healthy, apart from the occasional barked shin caused by stumbling in the dark over awkwardly stowed equipment.

Although it was tremendously hot and water was strictly rationed, they thrived on the cooking of Crilley, who had proved to be a culinary genius. Not only was he a dab hand at making pancakes but he managed, in the confines of his tiny galley, to transform rock-hard, dehydrated food pellets into tasty meals. Morale, which remained high, received a boost when they heard on Young's wireless that Italy had capitulated and the spirits of the nicotine addicts were further buoyed when Lyon relented and gave them permission to smoke when they were below decks in daylight hours.

The engine, too, played its part. The repaired shaft gave no trouble and apart from a slight hiccup caused by a faulty feedline when south of Lombok, the Gardner had purred sweetly under the watchful eye of Paddy McDowell and his off-sider, Boof Marsh. Although a most unlikely candidate for the job, the funloving, happy-go-lucky Boof, who was not put off in the slightest by the excessive heat in the engine room, had demonstrated a surprising degree of mechanical flair. However, such was Paddy's devotion to his mechanical baby that his enthusiastic apprentice was hardly ever given the chance to show off his skill.

Apart from the fright the middlewatchman received when a large tanker cut across *Krait*'s bows prior to a storm that struck on September 16, the rest of the journey to Bill Reynolds's old stamping ground at Pompong Island passed without incident. Although they had seen a number of native craft about, no one had bothered to come too close, nor investigate. Indeed, near Pelapis Island the sight of *Krait*'s Japanese flag had had the opposite effect, sending a small Malay fishing fleet scurrying off in all directions.

However, when they finally reached Pompong, which they had hoped to use as a base while searching for a suitable hideout for *Krait*, they were disappointed to find that the comings and goings of visiting fishermen made the island unsuitable. Not bothering to anchor they continued around the point, only to come face to face with what appeared to be an enemy vessel. Altering course 180 degrees, Carse slapped on full speed and ran for shelter, only to discover from the lookout positioned atop *Krait*'s mast that there was no cause for alarm. The Japanese patrol boat was nothing more than the wreck of *Kuala*. Poking sadly from the water, her mast rose like a skeletal obelisk, marking the place where so many had perished such a short time before.

Hoping that nearby Bengku Island (where some of the shipwrecked survivors from *Tien Kuang* had found sanctuary) might offer better shelter, they sailed eastwards and in so doing received their second fright of the day. As *Krait*'s dinghy was trying to find a gap in the seemingly impassable reef a Japanese float plane, apparently from the base at nearby Tjempa Island, suddenly appeared. While the men in the dinghy could do nothing more than sit tight, those on board *Krait* immediately dived for cover. However, the sight of the flag and the brown bodies, upon which stain had been recently reapplied, was evidently enough to reassure the pilot, who flew on, taking absolutely no notice of them.

That night, being unable to find a better place, they returned to Pompong, where they now hoped to remain until it was time to approach Durian Island (Lyon's old escape route camp), which had been selected as the rear folboat base. Anxious to make themselves as inconspicuous as possible now that they were so close to Singapore, they took the precaution of lowering the mast, an action that almost had disastrous consequences. Unskilled in a task that native fishermen are accustomed to performing with ease, the men lost control and gravity took over. Fortunately for Huston, who would have been almost certainly flattened had the heavy timbers hit the deck, it came to rest on the wheelhouse roof, smashing off the topmast. They were just clearing the debris away when the appearance of three natives in a small *kolek* — an old man and two boys — convinced them that before their luck ran out they should weigh anchor and move from the area as fast as possible.

As it was far too early in the day to approach Durian Island they detoured north, and, at about three in the afternoon, noticed small, hilly, uninhabited and jungle-covered Pandjang Island, which lay off the west coast of Rempang Island. Unable at this stage to either investigate the island further or alter the course towards Durian without attracting the attention of a nearby Japanese observation post on Galang Island, they headed towards the Bulan Straits to give the appearance that they were bound for Singapore. Unfortunately, such was the strategic placement of the enemy post that they were forced to continue on this northerly course. Consequently, when darkness descended, and with it a storm, they were still far away from their intended destination. Unsure whether Durian was still uninhabited and unwilling to take the risk of hitting uncharted reefs in the dark, Lyon abandoned the idea of using it as a base and issued orders to backtrack to Pandjang Island.

Lyon's decision to proceed no closer to Singapore came as a great relief for Carse, who had been apprehensive about the trip long before they had even reached Lombok Strait, let alone enemy territory. Now feeling decidedly edgy and with so many dangers lurking at every turn, darkness could not come quickly enough for the navigator. As the sun went down that night he muttered yet again a heartfelt 'Thank God' that he had survived another day.

With the newly selected base some kilometres from the original choice, the old plan possibly to hide *Krait* in Sumatra's Kampar River Estuary, an extensive waterway to the north of the Indragiri, was also scrapped. Furthermore, since Lyon now realised it was unrealistic to expect that *Krait*, no matter how well concealed, could remain undetected in one place for the best part of two weeks, any idea of finding a permanent hiding place was shelved. Calculating that a moving ship would be less likely to attract unwanted attention, he decided that *Krait* should wander about the waters of Borneo until it was time for the pick up.

Although they were back at Pandjang at 10 pm, having navigated a safe passage in the dark by the lights of fishing *pagars*, the positions of which Lyon had memorised, it was not until three hours later that they found a beach sheltered enough to attempt a landing. While Cobber Cain sounded the depth with a lead line, Carse edged the ship as close to the shore as he dared. As soon as the island had been reconnoitred by Davidson and Jones and declared to be suitable, Berryman and Marsh took turns to ferry the stores and the operatives ashore in the dinghy.

At about three o'clock, with the supplies and equipment safely stowed above the high water mark, it was time for Berryman, who had paddled the last load to the beach, to part company with Lyon and Huston, Page and Jones, Davidson and Falls — the six men who were to carry out the raid. With Singapore so close that he could see the city lights glowing on the horizon, it was especially hard for Berryman to say his final words of farewell. Bitterly disappointed, after all the months of training, that he and his reserve partner Boof Marsh were to be left behind, it was with understandable and overwhelming reluctance that he manoeuvred his dinghy out of the shallows and made his solitary journey back to *Krait*.

The raiding party did not expect to make contact with him, or indeed any of the others, until *Krait* returned to Pompong Island after dusk on October 1. Even then they knew it might be touch and go, for, if anything went wrong and the rendezvous was not kept by any or all of them, Lyon had given Carse orders to return to Australia immediately. As *Krait*, a dark, indistinct shadow on an inky black sea, faded from their sight to begin her perilous wandering, Lyon and his men wondered if they would ever see her again.

CHAPTER SEVEN

What Price Glory?

When dawn broke just over an hour later, *Krait*, which was heading in a south-westerly direction, was quite a distance from Pandjang and passing to the north of Pittong and Tortell Islands. Anxious to keep well away from the base camp, Carse continued in this direction for a considerable time before abruptly changing course for the Temiang Strait. With only eight men to run the ship and keep a round-the-clock watch, it was not long before they were all so dog-tired that the navigator was wondering if a few benzedrine tablets might not go amiss. However, as darkness approached and with it the open sea, Temiang and its numerous islands, around which too many dangers lurked for comfort, were left far behind, allowing them all to breathe a little more easily.

Although the relief after the non-stop strain of the previous thirty-six hours was welcome (indeed Carse equated it to spending 'an evening at home'), it was not long before all those on board realised that if there was something worse than too much activity it was too little. Apart from the boredom of aimlessly sailing nowhere in particular, there was the helpless frustration they felt at not knowing what was happening beyond their own small patch of ocean.

This uncertainty of what the future held affected members of the ship's company in quite different ways. Although Horrie Young, who spent most of his time at the wireless, eyed off the mass of plastic explosive perched upon it with some disquiet, he dismissed the period as 'uneventful'. Equally dismissive was Moss Berryman, whose days spent in almost non-stop lookout

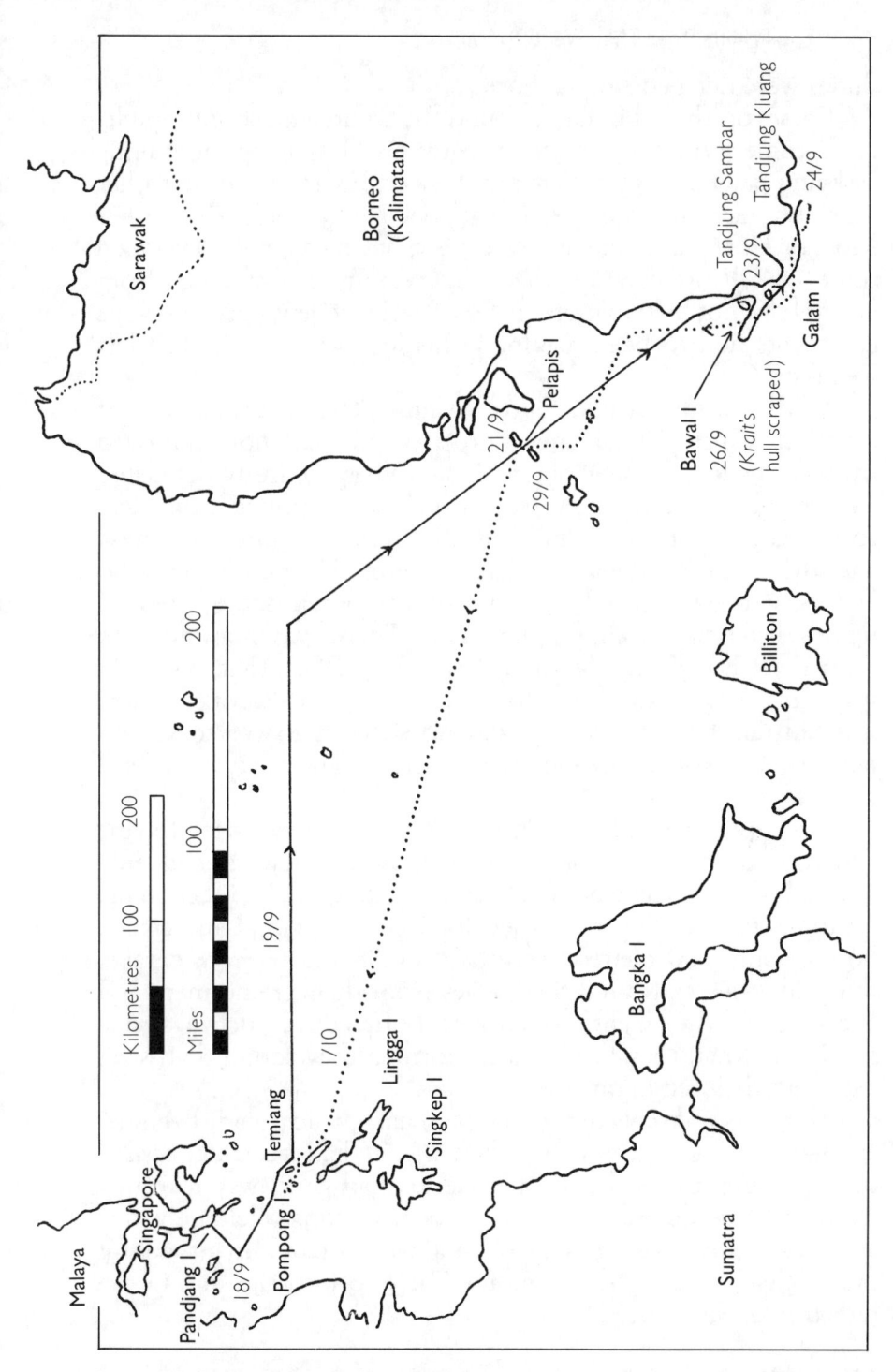

Map IV. Route taken by *Krait*, 18 September–1 October 1943, while the raiding party was away.

duties were deemed simply 'boring'.

Carse, on the other hand, found the strain almost unbearable. He became more toey as time progressed, describing the waiting as being far worse than that experienced by an expectant father outside a maternity ward. Although, being much older than either Moss or Horrie and, one would expect, having a better developed sense of self-preservation, his long period of abstinence from alcohol did not help matters, as was clearly evident in the nervous comments he had been making in his log ever since he had left Exmouth Gulf.

While some coped better than others, the sense of isolation which all of them experienced was not improved by their having to stay out to sea, well away from populated islands and native sailing vessels, which were spotted from time to time. As one shimmering day merged into the next and the night of the attack grew nearer, Horrie Young, who had now been relieved of most of his other duties, stepped up his listening watch on the radio. There was not much to report, although he learned from the BBC that the war was not progressing well for the enemy in Europe. There was nothing of local interest and no suggestion whatsoever on Japanese propaganda newscasts that the raiding party may have run into trouble.

On September 23, five interminably dull days after leaving Pandjang, the boredom of the late tropical evening was suddenly relieved when Carse, who had been navigating by dead reckoning, mistook the coastline of Borneo for low lying cloud and struck bottom only 200 metres from the shoreline. After considerable difficulty, they extricated themselves from their predicament and anchored for the night, only to be buffeted by such a strong swell that when they awoke next morning they found that *Krait* had drifted eleven kilometres.

They also discovered that the heat, which had been so excessive during the past few days that it had been impossible to walk barefoot on the wooden decks, had given way to rough weather. Consequently, after a day spent battling galeforce winds and seas, it was a very relieved Young who offered up a thankful prayer that the time had come for Carse to turn the ship in the direction of Singapore.

What Price Glory?

Throughout that night, acutely aware that the wee hours of the 25th was the earliest date for Lyon to launch the attack, Horrie strained his ears more keenly than ever for news of the raiders. Having been so severely sunburned on his backside that he was not able to sit down, this was no easy task, especially when the radio revealed that nothing seemed to be amiss. However, if nothing else, his vigil took his mind off his burnt rear-end and also off his stomach, which, because of reduced rations, was rumbling even more than usual.

With food stocks, and water in particular, running low, Andrew Crilley's pancakes were by now a mouth-watering memory. Gone too were such delicacies as steamed pudding, which had been replaced by a handful of raisins and a ship's biscuit, washed down by half a cup of water. Although they could do nothing about the diminishing food supply, the water problem was solved when it rained that night, bringing relief from the heat and replenishing the water casks. Not surprisingly, when the morning of September 27 dawned fine and clear above a glass-like sea, everyone was in an excellent frame of mind to jump overboard and scrape *Krait*'s hull.

The mass of green weed growing below the water line was so prolific that Paddy figured it was costing them at least half a knot. Since the ability to put as much distance between themselves and the Japanese in the least possible time might become very pressing in the near future, all hands were rallied.

It was a popular task and Moss Berryman, for one, had no objection to leaping into the tropical waters of the Java Sea, knife in hand, to relieve *Krait* of her unwanted underwater garden. As they dived and splashed and dangled fishing lines over the side, the war forgotten for the time being, they had no inkling that all hell had broken out in Singapore.

☠

From their hiding place high on jungle-covered Dongas Island, Lyon, Huston, Page and Jones could scarcely contain their elation.

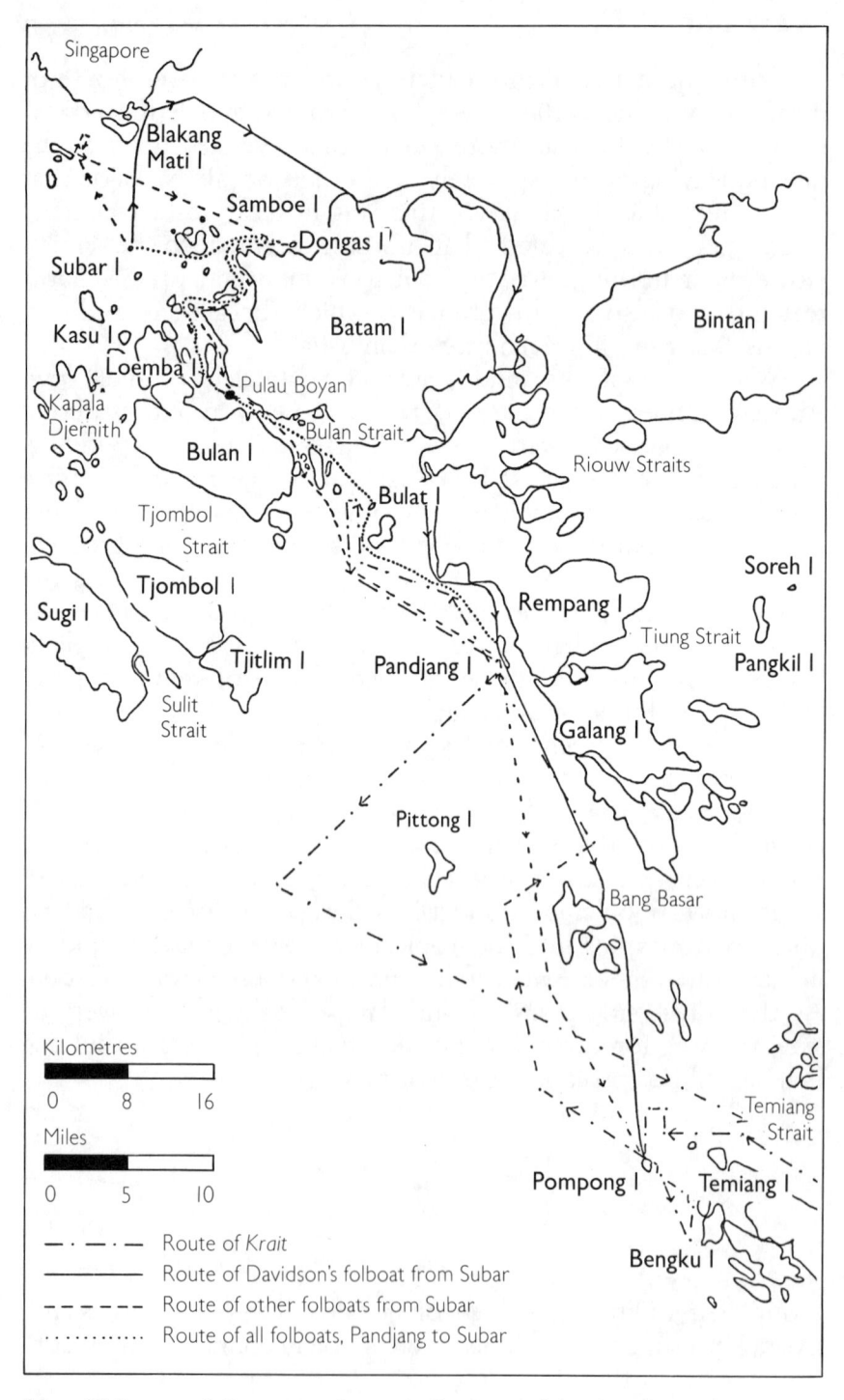

Map V. Route of Operation Jaywick, Pompong Island to Singapore.

What Price Glory?

As sirens wailed and Japanese patrol boats scurried to and fro in a frenzy of disorganised activity, they viewed with excitement the havoc their limpets had wrought. All seven sets of mines had exploded just before dawn, blowing up 37 000 tonnes of shipping, waking up the population on both sides of the strait and sending up a pall of black oily smoke, through which the bows of at least one sinking freighter could just be seen. As the raiders observed squadrons of aircraft leave Singapore's airfields to search in quite the wrong direction, they knew there was no doubt about it — Operation Jaywick had been one hundred per cent successful.

Not that it had been all plain sailing by any means. The trip up the Bulan Straits from Pandjang Island, where they had spent a few days resting and organising their gear, had been fraught with danger. Travelling only after dark, they had been so delayed on the second night by the need to skirt native fishing villages that when dawn broke they were still in a narrow part of the strait. Forced to go to ground, they had spent a most uncomfortable twelve hours lying in the mud of mosquito-infested mangroves, only metres from a busy village. Worse, when negotiating a tide-race Lyon's folboat had collided with Davidson's, so damaging the bow that he and Huston were having great difficulty keeping on course. Yet, in spite of the considerable energy being expended by this pair, the group made such excellent progress that they had reached the target area with days to spare.

Believing that the time could be put to good use by undertaking additional reconnaissance, Lyon had amended the plan. He headed not for Hill 120 — an elevated island known as Pulau Kapal Kechil which, because of its position overlooking Singapore Harbour, had been selected as the observation post — but to Pulau Dongas, an uninhabited island thirteen kilometres further east.

As a hide-out, Dongas was perfect and the view of the Roads anchorage from its elevated western end so superb that Lyon had decided to attack the ships moored there instead of those in the harbour area. Consequently, after a day's careful observation, they had set out on the night of September 24 loaded with limpets with which they intended to blow the targetted vessels to kingdom come.

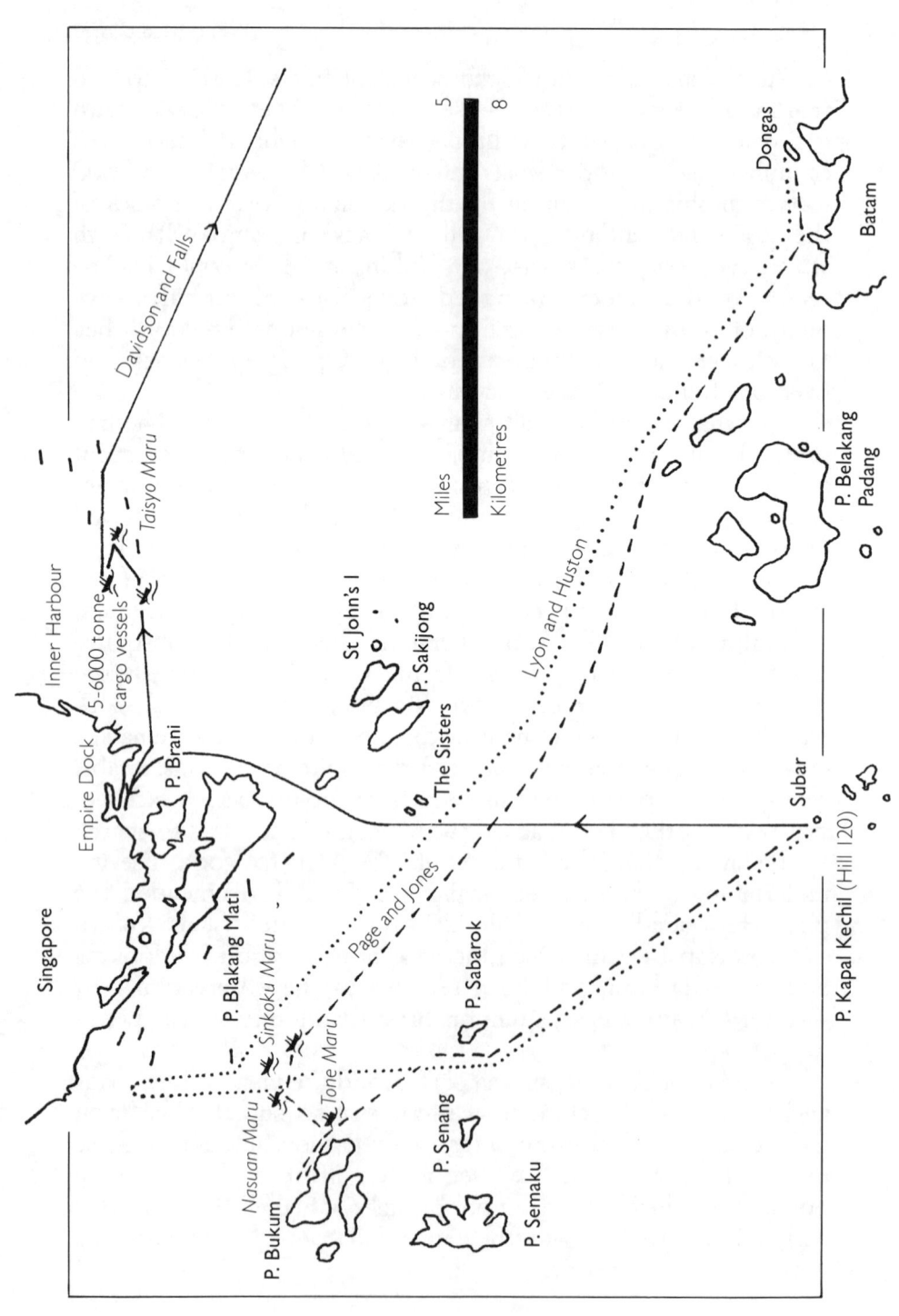

Map VI. The Attack courses for Operation Jaywick.

What Price Glory?

Unfortunately the tide, which swirled through the Singapore Straits at a fast rate of knots, had turned before they had reached their objective, propelling them backwards in the direction from which they had come and forcing them to abandon all thoughts of launching an attack. While the others retreated without any problems, Lyon and Huston, who were battling to make their way in their defective folboat, were caught in the open as the sun rose and only made it to the cover of Dongas's mangroves by the skin of their teeth.

Realising that any attack mounted from an easterly direction was doomed to failure, Lyon had reverted to his original plan and that night led his team back to Hill 120, only to discover, from the angry barking of a number of dogs, that it was inhabited. Yet all was not lost. Not far from Hill 120 was the tiny island of Subar — treeless, waterless and hideously hot, but ideally sited as an observation post.

After an appallingly uncomfortable day spent trying to keep cool and out of sight in the scant cover offered by the stiff, low-growing bracken, the men had set out that night for Singapore Harbour and the nine ships they had earmarked through the telescope for destruction. Although there were a few anxious moments for all three teams, their blackened faces and their black clothing rendered them almost invisible, allowing them to slip through the harbour defences undetected and place their deadly hardware in position.

In the end, only Jones and Page had managed to carry out their attack according to plan. Lyon and Huston, unable in the darkness to locate the now blacked-out freighters they had selected, decided to go for broke and placed all their limpets on an oil tanker, figuring that although the multi-compartmented vessel might not sink, it would undoubtedly make a spectacular blaze. Meanwhile Davidson and Falls, after careful reconnaissance, abandoned all idea of entering the well-lit dockyard area and opted instead to attach their explosives on three of the many ships lying in the Roads. As soon as the limpets were in place, all six had fled.*

---

*For a full and detailed account of the raiding party's experiences, see *The Heroes of Rimau* by Lynette Ramsay Silver, Sally Milner Publishing.

Lyon, Huston, Page and Jones had paddled for Dongas, where they planned to spend the day observing the results of their handiwork. They made it with only minutes to spare and had barely reached the safety of the mangroves when the first ship blew up. Meantime, Falls and Davidson, who because of their position could see nothing and heard only six of the seven explosions, sought refuge on Batam Island. As soon as it was dark, they made their way down the Riouw Straits and, forty-eight hours later, after detouring around numerous fishing stakes, were safely back at Pandjang. After tucking with relish into rations which they had had the foresight to secrete in a cave, they left a short note for Lyon before setting off on the last leg of their journey. Despite their being delayed by a violent storm, the pair made such good time that they reached Pompong Island with twenty-four hours to spare.

With growing tension they waited out the daylight hours of October 1. When night came and there was no sign of *Krait*, they did not worry themselves unduly, since the rendezvous was set for the twelve hours between dusk and dawn. However as the minutes, then hours, ticked by and the stars appeared with sparkling intensity in the velvety black sky, they began to wonder if indeed she was going to show up. After all, it was fourteen days since they had seen her — fourteen days in which anything may have happened. Midnight approached and there was still no sign of her. Where in the devil was she? Perhaps the engine had conked out. Perhaps the worst had happened and the crew was at this very minute in the hands of the dreaded Kempei Tai — the Japanese secret police. But before apprehension could give way to fear, *Krait*, a barely discernible shadow on an ebony sea, rounded the point with an abruptness that took them both by surprise.

Of the ten people involved in the subsequent joyous reunion, Carse was by far the most relieved. For him the past fortnight, and especially those last seven days, had been sheer torture and without a doubt the worst period in his life. Ever since the scraping of *Krait*'s hull things had begun to deteriorate. 'Heartily sick' from 'hanging about the coast of Borneo' and 'skulking by the by-ways and corners of the sea', Carse had become increasingly anxious about the return voyage through the Lombok Strait, so much so that his resolve had given way and he had taken to the rum supply. Had Berryman and Marsh, who had tumbled to his little secret, realised what it would later cost them, they would have allowed him the crutch upon which he was so obviously dependent.

Consequently, the last week of *Krait*'s voyage had been less than pleasant. While the 'younger' members of the crew felt the lash of Carse's tongue over what appear to have been imagined misdemeanours, he further vented his bad temper by writing derogatory remarks in the log to the effect that no one under the age of twenty-five should ever be selected for a voyage such as this. It is not surprising therefore that almost everyone was on edge as the date of the rendezvous had drawn nearer. And in the end, despite their counting off the hours and minutes, they had almost missed it.

Although Carse had held high hopes at three in the afternoon of September 29 of reaching Pompong in forty-seven hours, he had not reckoned with the weather. At eight o'clock on the morning of October 1, while they were still off the coast of Lingga Island, the clear blue sky had given way to leaden clouds and the silk-like sea was so chopped by angry wind-whipped waves that *Krait* was virtually stationary. Consequently at 7 pm on October 1, instead of being at Pompong as planned, they were still south of the Temiang Strait. It was not until fifteen minutes after midnight, over five hours late, that they had finally reached the rendezvous.

The realisation that only two of the six raiders were waiting came as a rude shock to Carse, who had planned to make a fast pick-up and disappear within the hour. When dawn broke and there was no sign of the others, he weighed anchor and headed for the Temiang Strait, intending to do precisely as ordered and sail for home. Davidson, however, had other ideas. Convinced that the other four were simply held up by the damaged folboat and the fierce storm he and Falls had encountered, he quietly canvassed the crew. Should they simply sail away and leave their comrades to an uncertain fate, or should they return and attempt a second rendezvous?

Not unexpectedly all except Carse voted to go back to Pompong. His dissention may have been a problem had Davidson, with the help of a discreet but well-positioned pistol, not persuaded him to change his mind. Having thus 'won' the co-operation of the navigator, Davidson then decreed that they should wait an extra day before returning to Pompong, so that the others had all the time they needed. With that settled, *Krait* and her crew set off for yet another bout of wandering, unaware that Lyon and the others had watched their departure that morning in absolute disbelief.

Although Davidson had been perfectly correct in his assumption that the damaged folboat and the storm had held them up, he had underestimated Lyon's determination to meet the deadline. Aware that the rendezvous could well mean the difference between death and survival, they had put in a superhuman effort, paddling the last forty-five kilometres in twenty-one hours and reaching Pompong with three hours to spare. Almost at the limit of their endurance, they had paddled about in the bay looking in vain for *Krait* before crashing into an exhausted sleep on the beach. At dawn, they had woken just in time to see her moving off toward the Temiang Strait.

Although Lyon immediately organised the group for a long stay, intending to obtain a native vessel and sail to India on the change of the monsoon, his plans went by the board when *Krait*, on the evening of October 3, returned. After a joyful reception, which saw the rum store broached, legally this time, *Krait* left Pompong and, much to Carse's relief, headed once more down the Temiang Strait.

Compared to the outward journey, which Lyon had found so dull, the homeward voyage through the Java Sea was unbelievably so. Indeed, such was the boredom that a lookout, comfortably nestled in a coil of rope atop the wheelhouse roof, fell asleep, incurring not only Lyon's displeasure but also the humiliation of being subjected to hard tack and water for three days, plus additional punishment.

As they entered Lombok Strait on October 11 the errant watchman was just returning to a normal diet when Ted Carse's worst fears were realised. They were spotted by a Japanese patrol boat.

She came out of the darkness from nowhere. One minute they were alone on the ocean, making tremendous headway

What Price Glory?

through the strait and believing that with the tide in their favour the worst was over, and the next she was almost upon them, white water creaming back from her bows as she altered course to intercept *Krait* on the port side.

The frantic calls of watchkeepers Joe Jones and Poppa Falls alerted the others, who grabbed their weapons and scurried to action stations behind the canvas awning, aware that their lives hung in the balance. They all knew that there was no question of their being taken alive. Although it was a perfectly legitimate ruse, to be found in enemy territory flying a Japanese flag would not be viewed favourably by the Japanese. Moreover, to open fire without revealing their true identity, thereby breaching international law, would almost certainly result in summary execution. Given the choice, it was better by far to die by their own hand than face the hideous prospect of prolonged torture and decapitation by the sword.

As the ship closed the gap, all those on *Krait* could see that although the vessel, which was flying no flags, was not overly large by naval standards her speed and her silhouette indicated she was either a Japanese minesweeper or a torpedo boat, both of which were more than capable of overtaking them. While Crilley, a devout Catholic, crouched in the stern and prayed for all he was worth, Moss Berryman stared at the rapidly advancing ship through the sights of his Bren, all but convinced that the chances of ever tucking into another plate of his mother's apple pie and cream were very remote indeed. Below decks in the Officer's Mess, Davidson calmly made final preparations to detonate enough plastic explosive to blow them sky high, while Lyon, who was in the wheelhouse with Carse, stood by to hand out the suicide pills.

Not a muscle moved on board *Krait*. As the Jaywick men watched in absolute silence, scarcely daring to breathe, the sleekly built enemy vessel, which was now so near that they could see her crew standing on the deck, began to pace the smaller ship, which was less than one-third her size. Just when all appeared to be lost and those on *Krait* had resigned themselves to imminent death, the Japanese vessel broke off its pursuit of *Krait* and abruptly altered course.

Why she did so will remain forever a mystery, but it is

probably a fair bet that the late hour and the Officer-of-the-Watch's desire to withdraw to the comfort of his bunk, rather than investigate the credentials of a grotty little fishing boat flying a Japanese flag, most probably had something to do with it.

After this hair-raising encounter, Carse declared that their subsequent battle with the ferocious tide as they made their way through Lombok was 'like sitting before a nice fire'. Always disturbed by the sight of the Japanese flag fluttering on *Krait*'s stern, his relief became absolute the next night when Lyon ordered the offending article, now looking even worse for wear, to be taken down for the last time.

Given his edginess and nervous apprehension throughout the voyage, Carse's extraordinary behaviour not twenty-four hours later is mystifying. Perhaps his overwhelming sense of relief at having survived the passage through the straits, coupled with his desire to flex what he believed to be his rightful authority, prompted Carse to throw caution to the wind and place all their lives at risk. Evidently very put out that he, a navy man, was subservient to an army officer — and a Pommie one at that — on what was definitely an ocean-going exercise, he had Horrie Young transmit a signal to Exmouth Gulf. Perhaps in an effort to make his part in the operation appear more important than it was, he had arranged to send the code word 'Potshot' to one of his cronies if Lombok Strait was patrolled. Why Carse thought this information was of such importance to break radio silence when he could deliver a message in person in a few days' time is a matter that has never been explained. One thing, however, is certain. When Lyon discovered that security had been breached while still in range of Japanese aircraft, he was livid.

Fortunately, no harm was done. Although the wireless station could not be raised, the unauthorised message was evidently too brief to allow the enemy time to get a fix on it. Two days later, with the Japanese no longer a threat and with the full approval of his commanding officer, Horrie tapped out a message that gave *Krait*'s expected time of arrival, followed by the two words everyone in SRD had been longing to hear — 'Mission completed'.

They arrived at Exmouth Gulf early on the morning of October 19, thereby ending a voyage that had taken them almost six and a half thousand kilometres in forty-eight days. The safe return of the ship sparked emotions that were as diverse as those who experienced them. While Horrie was thankful that the 'nightmare' was over and Moss wanted nothing more for the time being than a large slice of apple pie, the irrepressible Boof Marsh rejoiced in the knowledge that they had 'flown the Rising Sun' and got away with it.

On the other end of the scale was Lyon — the cool-headed, icy-calm and professional soldier who viewed Jaywick as nothing more than a well-executed raid that had gone according to plan. Unfortunately, while this was undeniably true, the fact that the raid had gone so well was to prompt a most unexpected reaction from both the Allied High Command and the Japanese.

When it was realised that the enemy had no idea who was responsible for blowing up the ships in Singapore Harbour Lyon's superiors decided to keep Jaywick's success a secret, since similar raids might ensue. Although propaganda had been one of the operation's main aims, this decision ensured that the chance to create panic in every Japanese-held port in South East Asia was lost, as was the opportunity to lift the morale of the Australian and British people at a time when Allied successes were few and far between. In short, the clampdown on security had reduced Operation Jaywick, surely one of the most daring raids in history, to nothing more than an exclusive, if spectacular, sideshow.

Tragic as this loss of propaganda may have been, a far greater tragedy was unfolding elsewhere. In Singapore the mysterious attack on harbour shipping had sparked off an internal enquiry that had degenerated into a hideous reign of terror. Determined to discover the identity of those who had masterminded what was believed to be an outrageous act of internal sabotage, Tokyo had ordered the Kempei Tai to investigate the matter.

On October 10, the tenth day of the tenth month, the hated secret police had swooped upon the hapless civilian population. Victims were dragged from their beds in the dead of night never to return, while others, broken and battered from bouts of prolonged torture, were flung into vermin-infested dungeons to die slowly from starvation and neglect. Within weeks of the advent of the 'Double Tenth Massacre', hundreds of innocent Chinese, Malays and European internees would be dead, tortured beyond endurance or barbarically executed by Kempei Tai determined to find out who was responsible for such an immense loss of face.

It would be years before ordinary Australians learned the truth — that the price paid for Operation Jaywick was one of the bloodiest of the entire war.

CHAPTER EIGHT

Becalmed in Darwin

After the high tension and excitement of the past six weeks, *Krait*'s safe arrival back in Australia was something of a let down. Exmouth Gulf, being remotely situated, had little to offer the crew in the way of entertainment and, with Jaywick declared top-secret, what should have been a triumphal return was by necessity very low-key. Indeed, such was the security clamp-down that, with the exception of a small dinner party hosted by US Admiral Christie at Potshot for Lyon and Page before they flew south for debriefing, there was no celebration whatsoever. Although Morris had an unexpected change of scenery when he sailed to Perth on *Chanticleer* to receive attention for his still unhealed ankle, the rest of the crew had no such reprieve. For the best part of three weeks, while *Krait* received urgent repairs to make her seaworthy enough to proceed to Darwin, they cooled their heels at Potshot.

Consequently, Lyon and Page were somewhat astonished by the reception they received from the top brass when they arrived in Melbourne and then Sydney. Although the existence of Jaywick was known to only a select few, the congratulations were so embarrassingly effusive that the pair were glad to deliver their reports and escape back to the relative sanity of the Northern Territory. They arrived in Darwin on November 3, three days ahead of *Krait*, which had sailed from Exmouth Gulf under the command of Donald Davidson.

Security was still tight, so much so that *Krait* tied up, not in Darwin harbour itself, but in the secluded East Arm, about five kilometres by water and twenty by road from Darwin township. Here, on a small island linked to the mainland by a causeway, was a secret base known only by its undercover name of Lugger Maintenance Section, or LMS. Surrounded by mangroves and housed well away from curious eyes in buildings formerly occupied by the Darwin Quarantine Station, the LMS was an efficient operation run by AIB.

Used primarily as a staging post and supply depot for Allied undercover units, it also organised and repaired seaborne transport and processed people who had been evacuated or rescued from Japanese-held islands to the north of Australia. Although LMS was the brainchild of ISD's Major Mott, who had set it up in November 1942 when Cairns's Z Experimental Station had started to burst at the seams, it had passed to AIB's control during the organisational shake-up in early 1943, when ISD became SRD. Such was the security at LMS that none of the many who passed through it, nor any of the RAAF personnel attached to the adjoining flying boat base, had any idea that it was anything other than a Quarantine Station.

Perhaps the remoteness of the base, which was kilometres from the nearest pub, was the catalyst that now caused Paddy McDowell to blot his copybook. In what can only be described as a woeful lapse of self-control, Paddy, whose behaviour up until now had been exemplary, broached the ship's liquor supply and became rip-roaringly drunk. Although Lyon conceded that Paddy was an excellent engineer, his drinking spree caused such a ruction that Lyon reluctantly informed SRD that he had no further use of his services.

Paddy's lack of restraint did not, however, have any bearing on Lyon's report on his conduct during Operation Jaywick. Although Carse's behaviour on the mission and the acerbic comments he had written in the log about 'the younger members of the crew' ensured that neither he, nor those whom he had criticised, could receive anything more than an MID (Mention in Despatches), Paddy's devotion to duty was fully recognised. When the awards were handed out the following year he became the proud possessor of a Distinguished Service Medal, an honour also bestowed upon operatives Wally Falls, Joe Jones and Andrew Huston. Officers Lyon, Page and Davidson received Distinguished Service Orders while Taffy Morris and Andrew Crilley were each awarded the Military Medal.

However, as these awards were some months off, no one, other than the officers, had any inkling of the high regard in which they and their mission were held by the military establishment. Nor were they aware that Jaywick's outstanding success had triggered off ambitious plans for similar raids, or that Lyon would recall some of them the following year to take part in another attack on Singapore Harbour, to be code named Operation Rimau. Consequently, on November 10 as soon as the team had been released from the clutches of intelligence officers in Darwin, they were flown to Brisbane for a slap-up party before going their separate ways — Lyon to organise Operation Hornbill, which would later evolve into Rimau; Davidson to set up a Commando School at Fraser Island, off the Queensland coast; and the others to return either to SRD or normal duties. Only *Krait* remained in Darwin. As soon as she had arrived, LMS, knowing how vital a role she had played in Operation Jaywick, had grabbed her for future covert missions.

With the safe return of the vessel from Singapore and the excellent results obtained by the Jaywick team, Special Operations had come to the conclusion that seaborne raids, using ships which were common to South East Asian waters, were the way to go. As a result, plans were already in train to build a number of Indonesian-type fishing boats to carry other raiding parties deep into enemy territory.

Had the military strategists known, as they pored over their maps and blueprints, that there was more to Operation Jaywick than met the eye, they may have concentrated their energies elsewhere. In Singapore, not only were countless civilians still paying a terrible price for the raid, but the Japanese had already salvaged and were returning to service no less than five of the seven ships. Unfortunately, for the SRD's planning department, this information was not at this stage available. The chilling facts of the Double Tenth Massacre would not be revealed until after the war, while the ultimate fate of the ships would not be uncovered for a further forty-five years.

Consequently, plans for the fleet of pseudo-Asian craft went ahead. Indeed, such was the faith being placed in the ability for other vessels to do what *Krait* had done that orders had been issued to spare no expense in either their construction or in their outfitting. Although the vessels, known as 'Country Craft', would appear to be outwardly identical to native-style sailing ships, there the similarity would end. Not only would they carry a camouflaged armament, they would also be supplied with powerful diesel engines to eliminate the reliance on wind.

Since the native vessels on which the Country Craft were to be based were never built to formal plans, SRD had eventually produced an acceptable design by combining the scant amount of information available in the Melbourne Public Library with that gleaned from *Yachting*, a popular sailing magazine. Dubbed 'Snake Class' in deference to *Krait*, the ships were described loosely as 'Singaporean Junks'. As the first of these snake ships had been earmarked for Operation Rimau and the rest had not moved much past the planning stage, LMS, being unable to find any other typically Asian vessels, had seized the initiative and appropriated *Krait*.

Unfortunately, owing to the lack of craft and what amounted to a demarcation dispute between the RAN and AIB over the control, manning and financing of AIB vessels, the operational side of LMS did not live up to expectations. SRD's 'fleet' consisted of only one vessel — *Krait* — until February 1944 when HMAS *Alatna*, a sea-ambulance launch of twenty-eight tonnes skippered by Ted Carse and with Cobber Cain as one of the six-man crew, arrived from Sydney, and a small launch named *Heather* was temporarily borrowed from the RAN.

Despite high hopes, *Alatna* and *Krait* were to see little action. Although it was planned to send *Krait* into New Guinea waters in January, the inability of the RAN and AIB to resolve their differences put paid to her leaving Darwin. While Paddy McDowell might have thought it a great idea, the outrageous suggestion put forward to the RAN by SRD's senior naval officer, one Commander Branson RN, to use *Krait* and *Alatna* as 'Q' ships to bait enemy submarines, was treated with the contempt it deserved. Fortunately, since there were few clandestine parties requiring seaborne transportation at that time, AIB was able to obtain either Allied submarines or small craft from the RAN's flotilla to take them behind enemy lines.

It was not until March 1944 that *Krait*, which had been sitting idle since November, was assigned to Mugger project and, with the demarcation dispute mercifully settled, was given the chance to strut her stuff. As the aim of Mugger was to establish a series of supply dumps and bases which would facilitate the insertion and maintenance of parties in enemy-controlled Timor, Sumba and Sabu Islands, *Krait*, *Alatna* and *Heather* were an integral part of the project.

On March 25, while the other two vessels explored the possibility of using various reefs and islets in the Timor Sea as supply dumps, *Krait* sailed for the Kimberley region in search of a site for the main base. After examining and rejecting for one reason or another several localities, including Cassini Islet and the Maret Group, *Krait*'s CO, Lieutenant Witt, settled on an inlet at Cape Voltaire, near Yampi Sound, which he named Krait Bay. In early May, as soon as the base, known as Hornet, had finished being provisioned, *Krait* (which for administrative purposes had been commissioned into the RAN on April 5 and now gloried in the title HMAS *Krait*) returned to Darwin.

Evidently the sea voyage, after so many months of inactivity, was too much for both *Krait* and *Alatna*. Plagued by engine trouble, which was further aggravated by a lack of spare parts, they were out of commission for almost two months. With the ships vital to the plan, the entire Mugger project came to an abrupt and indefinite halt prompting the skippers of both vessels, plus a number of the crew, to request a return to regular service. Apparently they figured that anything had to be better than sitting in the sweltering heat of Darwin doing absolutely nothing.

Finally, on July 1, both vessels were ready to go to sea. *Krait* departed at once to set up dumps on Browse and Sandy Islands in readiness for a mission known as Wasp, while *Alatna*, which had been given a similar task for a party code-named Apache, headed for Ashmore Reef. However, any relief that the Mugger project was back on course was short-lived when *Krait* and *Alatna* both signalled that bad weather had stopped play. Although *Krait* was handicapped by a number of mechanical problems, including a complete failure of the pumps (which resulted in all the stores being saturated with seawater) and a wireless operator so overcome with seasickness that his life was endangered, she ultimately completed her task on July 19. When she finally limped

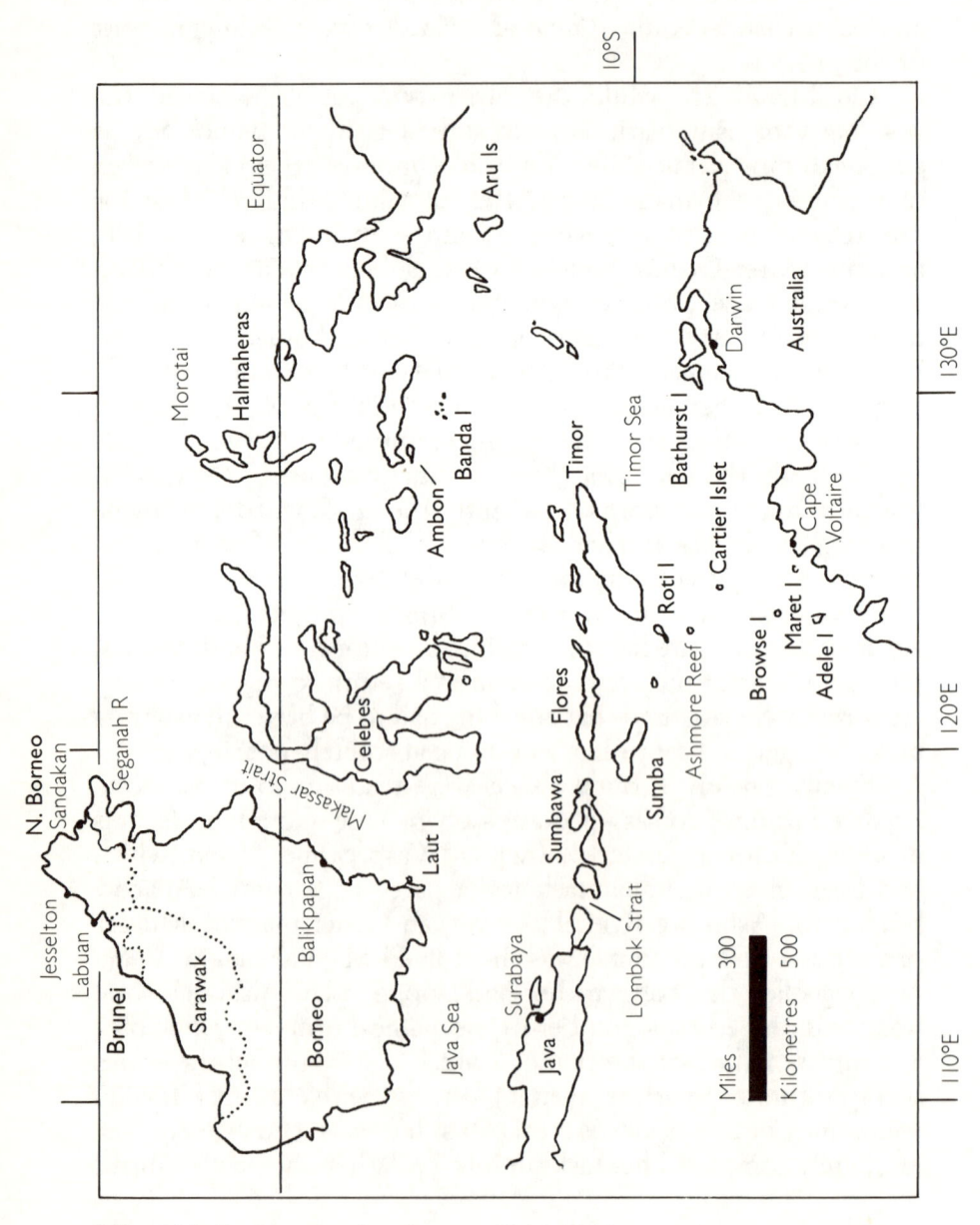

Map VII. *Krait*'s area of operation, 1944–1964.

back to Darwin five days later, she was in need of a complete dockyard overhaul.

SRD could be forgiven for thinking that the Mugger project was jinxed. *Krait*, with spare parts for her gearbox and pumps unprocurable, her hull opening up and no proper facilities for carrying out a major refit, was out of commission indefinitely; her newest CO, Skipper Naylor, had been hospitalised with a severe skin rash that would see him confined to bed for weeks; and *Alatna*'s latest commanding officer, Lieutenant Bruno Reymond (the third appointment to the vessel since February), came down with a case of mumps almost immediately on his arrival in July.

By this stage, SRD had had enough. On August 15 Hornet base was closed down and the entire Mugger project, with its subdivisions of Operations Wasp, Gnat, Apache, Bat, Flea and Louse, was cancelled. *Alatna*, which had been forced by engine failure to abort a planned reconnaissance of Roti Island near Timor in preparation for Operation Gnat, was recalled. When the problem was rectified, she was dispatched to Hornet under the command of Lieutenant Adamson (skipper number four) to bring back the base personnel and the bulk of the stores, only to suffer another engine breakdown which put her out of action for the foreseeable future. Meanwhile, Lieutenant Reymond, whose command of *Alatna* had been usurped by Adamson, had been given a new job: in what would prove to be one of the most tragic twists of fate he accepted an appointment to join Ivan Lyon on Operation Rimau — a decision that would ultimately cost him his life.

Although Mugger was resurrected under the name of Operation Sounder in September, it was a lost cause. With *Alatna*, as well as *Krait*, unserviceable and the Country Craft, on which SRD had pinned such high hopes, delayed indefinitely by a lack of skilled labour, disputes, go-slows and a shortage of materials, it was impossible to carry out any further missions. Although *Karinya*, a fast-supply vessel, had been promised she had failed to materialise, leaving LMS without any alternative transport.

With no vessels and no operations planned, activity ground to a halt. By late November, with only one officer, Flight Lieutenant Brierley, and four Timorese nationals on the staff, the base was like a ghost town.

Such was the air of depression it was just as well that no one connected with Special Operations had any idea that disaster had overtaken, or was about to overtake, almost every person ever connected with *Krait*.

They would have been devastated to know that Lyon and Davidson were already dead. Unable to evade the Japanese after the Rimau team had successfully attacked shipping in Singapore Harbour on the morning of October 11, their corpses now lay on two small islands in the Riouw Archipelago. Lyon had perished as he had lived, dying in a blaze of glory at Soreh Island after holding off more than a hundred Japanese troops. His 2IC, Donald Davidson, wounded and unable to leave the nearby and uninhabited Tapai Island, had used his cyanide capsule to take his own life, lest he reveal under torture the whereabouts of his comrades.

Ultimately, his sacrifice, and that of the young corporal with him, would prove to be in vain. Hounded by the Japanese, the rest of the Rimau party, including the other four Jaywick veterans, would be either killed or captured before the year was out. Andrew Huston would perish near Buaja Island on December 16, while less than a month later his best mate, Boof Marsh, would die of wounds and neglect in gaol in Singapore. Bob Page and Wally Falls, captured with Marsh, would be held in appalling conditions for seven months before being beheaded on 7 July 1945 with another eight of the party. Not even Bruno Reymond, whose inopportune attack of the mumps had seen him transferred at the last minute from *Alatna* to Operation Rimau, would survive. On December 21, while attempting to flee to safety in a hijacked junk, he would be knocked unconscious by his Chinese captives and tossed over the side to drown.*

However, since intercepted Japanese signals which would alert SRD to the tragic outcome of Operation Rimau had not yet been decoded, and with the Country Craft supposedly back on track, SRD's plans for future incursions into enemy territory went ahead as scheduled. In order to maintain more efficient control of these

---

*For a detailed account of Operation Rimau, see *The Heroes of Rimau* by Lynette Ramsay Silver, Sally Milner Publishing.

Becalmed in Darwin

and existing operations, SRD decided to establish at LMS a special headquarters known as 'Group D'. Under the command of Major Seymour Bingham, this unit was to be responsible for all missions south of the Java, Flores and Banda Seas. As a result, just when it appeared that the LMS must surely die a natural death, the ailing base was given a new lease of life in December 1944.

Despite no Country Craft being yet in sight and both *Krait* and *Alatna* being declared useless, Group D was quite active in the early months of 1945. Although it was not nearly as busy as Group C, which was organising Operations Semut and Agas, the first phases of which were to be dropped by air into Borneo in March, Group D was responsible for ensuring that Lagarto and Cobra, two SRD parties which had been operating in Timor for some time, continued to receive regular supply drops from the RAAF.

It was fortunate that the Air Force was able to continue to place aircraft at SRD's disposal, for the Country Craft were a long time coming. *Tiger Snake* was the first of these vessels, each of which had cost a massive 82 000 pounds to build and outfit. Her construction had been completed far too late for Operation Rimau (which had been obliged to make other and far from satisfactory arrangements).

She eventually arrived in late January after a voyage from Fremantle that her commanding officer, Lieutenant Witt (*Krait*'s former skipper), would long remember. After two months of sea trials off the southern WA coast, she had set off for Darwin on January 7, only to turn back in the early hours of the following morning with engine trouble. As she had neared the shore her unfamiliar silhouette, caught in the beam of the searchlights, had alarmed the shore battery, which opened fire. Fortunately their aim was off and *Tiger Snake*, after hurriedly identifying herself, was able to return to port unscathed.

With her mechanical problems allegedly rectified, she set off again on January 13 — a date that would prove to be most inauspicious. Constantly delayed by engine failures, which saw her resort to hoisting her sails, it was not until twelve wearisome days later that she arrived in Darwin.

Her momentous, if much delayed, arrival prompted SRD to

revamp the long-abandoned Mugger project, now renamed Sunfish. So pleased was SRD to see *Tiger Snake* that the ship was sent out of the harbour under full sail on February 5 to allow an airborne photographer to record the event for posterity. With the photographs satisfactorily taken she left Darwin the following day, bound for Ashmore Reef to cache supplies for operatives attached to the Mugger/Sunfish project. By March 11 *Tiger Snake* had visited the reef three times to deliver stores and supplies — a process that it was estimated could have been completed in one-third of the time had the engine not kept breaking down. Less than a month later, having received[1] orders to proceed to SRD's recently established advance base at Morotai, the most northerly island of the Moluccas Group, she was gone.

Although LMS had been promised five Country Craft by this time, only one, *River Snake*, had arrived. As the Sunfish project was still going ahead, this lack of craft was something of a problem. *Krait*, which had finally been repaired and now sported a new canvas canopy and side curtains, as well as compass, was busy taking stores out to HMAS *Coongoola*, moored off West Bay in the Kimberley region, while *Alatna* was still inoperable, owing to a bent crankshaft and leaky plywood hull. With no other ships available and the long-awaited *Karinya* now stuck in Brisbane with engine troubles, *River Snake* was given the much postponed job of reconnoitring Japanese-controlled Roti Island for Suncharlie — a coastwatching party attached to the Sunfish project.

The ship arrived at Roti, via Ashmore Reef, on April 23 without incident but as she sailed along the coast towards the entry point, a strong current slowed her progress considerably. Since *River Snake* was indistinguishable from an authentic Indonesian vessel, this would have been of no consequence had not the Australian ensign (which for some inexplicable reason had not been removed) come unfurled. Too late someone noticed that it was flapping in the stiff breeze, advertising to all and sundry the ship's true origins. Believing that the planned four-day land reconnaissance would now be impossible, it was decided to make do by carrying out a lightning raid on a village in the hope of capturing natives for interrogation.

The ease with which the raiding party captured two natives

Becalmed in Darwin

from a small village was evidently the reason why the party leader had a sudden change of heart. *River Snake* had only gone as far as Ashmore Reef on the return journey to Darwin when it was decided to put about and carry out the land reconnaissance as had been planned.

It would have been better had they gone straight home. Almost immediately things began to go wrong. For a start the terrain was too difficult for the landing party to achieve its objective and before long its presence, not surprisingly, was known to the Japanese. Then, while attempting to elude one of the search parties, the native prisoner whom they had taken ashore as a guide escaped and it was only with the utmost difficulty that the remainder managed to make the rendezvous with *River Snake*. And when they finally interrogated their remaining captive, they discovered he was unable to divulge any useful information.

If those involved in this less than successful mission were apprehensive about the reactions of their superiors, they need not have worried. By the time *River Snake* returned to Darwin, SRD had received a piece of news so alarming that by comparison the Suncharlie fiasco faded into insignificance.

To SRD's horror, it had learned that the Lagarto party was almost certainly in enemy hands in Timor. Furthermore, because of its gross incompetence in not supplying Lagarto's signaller with a foolproof security check to alert them that he had been captured and was transmitting under duress, SRD personnel had not detected that all signals sent since October 1943 had been controlled by the Japanese. In response to these signals, SRD had not only dropped food, ammunition, supplies and stores to the enemy for almost two years, it had also divulged unauthorised and ultra-secret information and sent in two other parties to Timor, one of which was known to be missing. Since there was no other way of confirming whether the sickening deductions about Lagarto were true or not, SRD decided that a party would have to be secretly inserted into Timor to investigate.

Therein lay the stumbling block. Although it was easy enough to drop the party into Timor by parachute once air transport had been made available, getting it out again by ship was quite another matter.

Despite the fact that engineers had promised that by late April *Krait*, having returned from her excursion to West Bay, would be ready for operations, she was not. Nor was she equipped in any way to undertake a mission as risky as this. Indeed, the RAN had decreed that the vessel was quite unsuitable for any operational work which entailed carrying additional personnel or proceeding beyond sheltered waters — an opinion shared by a representative of SRD who had recommended the ship be relegated to harbour duties. Evidently Group D thought otherwise: *Krait* would sail to Timor. However, before any such venture could be contemplated a silent underwater exhaust would have to be fitted, the wireless transmitter rewired and, since there were no escort vessels available, she would also need to be armed.

Time went by. May came and went with no sign of the weapons that had been urgently requested. With neither the RAN nor anyone else being able to spare escort vessels for the job and with no aircraft available, the investigation into Lagarto's activities in Timor was put on hold.

On June 6 two .5 calibre Colt Browning machine guns finally arrived. Two days later they had been installed on *Krait*'s specially strengthened deck and firing tests had been completed to the satisfaction of her commanding officer, Sub-Lieutenant Harry Williams. However, despite the urgent nature of the mission, it was not for another twenty days that *Krait* received orders to proceed to Bathurst Island to carry out beach-landing exercises with a rubber dinghy in preparation for the operation.

On the last day of June, as soon as she arrived back in Darwin, Williams submitted a report requesting an immediate upgrading of the engine-room ventilation. During the exercise it had been discovered that, in order to accommodate all the men needed for the operation, the hatches on the engine-room housing had to be closed, starving the engineers below of fresh air.

However urgent Williams considered the ventilation work to be, there was no time for such refinements. With a plane suddenly available, the three-man investigation team, code-named Sunlag and headed by Group D's Captain A.D. Stevenson, had already parachuted into Timor. On July 9, having learned from signals sent by Stevenson that Lagarto was in Japanese hands, SRD ordered the evacuation of the Sunlag team. With the extraction point a considerable distance from the party, a rendezvous was arranged with *Krait* for the night of July 15 and, if necessary, for the next three nights, between the hours of 10 pm and 2 am.

The date chosen for *Krait*'s departure from Darwin — Friday July 13 — was, from an astrological point of view, ill-advised. As the ship approached the Timor coast on the night of the 15th, the weather conditions deteriorated alarmingly. Deciding that the poor visibility and rough seas would greatly limit the possibility of sighting Sunlag's signals, let alone allow the crew to manoeuvre the rubber dinghy safely to shore, Lieutenant Williams aborted the rendezvous and took *Krait* out to sea.

The next night they tried again. This time, as *Krait* approached the coast, several lights were spotted. Wishing to cut engine noise to the minimum, Williams reduced the ship's speed to dead slow. As a result, *Krait* did not reach the rendezvous position in time and put out to sea without any contact being made.

The third attempt on the night of July 17 was no better. Although the weather was initially good, by 1 am visibility was down to less than thirty metres, making it impossible to see Sunlag's signals and forcing *Krait* once more out to sea. Mindful that the next attempt would be the final chance to make contact, the crew tried again the following night. At 1.40 am, with only twenty minutes to go until the time limit ran out, they were rewarded by the sight of Sunlag's morse signal (the letter 'R') flashing from the shore. As Williams eased the ship to within three hundred metres of the beach, her crew was in no doubt that the operation must go without a hitch. They were so close to land that not only could they quite plainly see enemy vehicles travelling up and down the coastal road, but they could also hear the sound of music and voices wafting out across the water. As *Krait*'s engineer Seaman Sid O'Dwyer later recalled, it was like being 'Peeping Toms at a window'.

Evidently the gravity of the situation did not make much impression on SRD's rescue party. In what appears to be an abysmal lack of foresight, the rescue team, which consisted of Major T.C. Johnson (British Army), Lieutenant J.W. Jeffray (RNVR), Captain Bullock (British Army) and Warrant Officer W.F. Doddrill (AIF), was nowhere near ready. For a start the rubber boat had not been prepared and sixteen vital minutes passed before they were able to launch it. There was then a lengthy delay while party leaders Johnson and Jeffray, who had been asleep on the engine-room housing, organised themselves. While an incredulous Sid O'Dwyer watched the major bedeck himself with enough equipment, hand grenades and other weapons, including a dagger stuck down the side of his sock, to storm the beaches at Normandy, Lieutenant Jeffray scrabbled around, trying to find his gear in the dark.

Since O'Dwyer had taken the precaution of ensuring that the ship remained blacked out by removing all the light fuses, the lieutenant decided that some alternative form of illumination was required. Before any one could stop him, he had whipped out a torch which he then proceeded to flash around in an effort to locate his equipment. O'Dwyer, seeing the light, burst out of the engine room like an enraged bull, pitched the torch over the side and let forth a stream of abuse which left no one in any doubt as to what he thought of the errant officer's parentage.

With all the delays, it was after half past two before the rescue team was ready to leave the ship. Major Johnson, festooned like a Christmas tree, stepped off the deck straight into the water. Hindered by the weight of his assorted ironmongery, he sank like a stone and was only saved from a watery grave by the fast action of Warrant Officer Doddrill, who being a practical and cool-headed member of SRD's instructional staff, jumped in after him and hauled him to the surface with a rope. It was not until 2.40 am, forty-four minutes after launching the dinghy, that the rescue team actually left the ship's side.

A desperate and risky attempt by Williams at a quarter past two, to try to attract Sunlag's attention and make amends for the mission's appalling display of ineptitude, failed utterly. At 2.42 am, two minutes after the dinghy had left, the shore signals stopped and contact was lost. Forty minutes later the dinghy, which when it failed to answer *Krait*'s recognition signals was almost blown out of the water, returned to the ship.

If those on *Krait* hoped that Sunlag had been rescued, given the length of time the dinghy had been away, they were to be sorely disappointed. With no shore signals to guide them, the boat party had lost its sense of direction and had not even made it to the shallow water. Indeed, it was only by sheer chance that they had relocated *Krait* in the darkness. At 3.25 am, when a further signal attempt failed to raise Sunlag (which, having no idea that *Krait* was just off the beach, had long since retreated from its perilous position), *Krait* left for Darwin.

With barely any food remaining from their eight-day ration pack the unfortunate Sunlag party spent the next eighteen days dodging Japanese and scrounging food from native villages until the RAN took the initiative and mounted a rescue from Darwin. At 6.15 on the morning of August 5, Harbour Defence Motor Launch 1324, commanded by Ray Evans, showed how it should have been done. With the corvette HMAS *Parkes* under the command of Lieutenant N.O. 'Paddy' Vidgen standing off the coast and fighter aircraft on immediate standby in Darwin, the launch approached the rendezvous point. Thirty minutes later the rescue team was back on board, having extracted the entire party (including a native Timorese that Sunlag wished to interrogate) in a rubber dinghy, without mishap. Although it was later claimed that *Krait*'s operation had been hindered by poor weather conditions and the efficiency of the personnel involved impaired by drenchings from 'spray and seawater', SRD denounced the bungling as 'inexcusable'.

Unfortunately, the long delay in rescuing Sunlag had tragic consequences. Two days after its arrival in Darwin the party's signaller, Sergeant R.G. Dawson, died from kidney failure — the result of an obscure infection contracted through injuries sustained to his feet when the party, in order to leave no trail for the pursuing Japanese, had been forced to remove their heavy boots and go barefoot.

The failure of her rescue mission, coupled with the July 21 report submitted by Lieutenant Williams on his return to Darwin, ensured that the Timor episode was *Krait*'s operational swansong. According to Williams the voyage had been a calamity from start to finish: the generator had packed up; the bilge pumps had failed; water had entered the wireless room hatch, temporarily rendering the wireless inoperable; the propeller shaft had developed an alarming vibration; and the wheelhouse had started to fall apart, allowing rainwater to enter. To top it off, the ventilation in the engine room, already a contentious issue, was so poor that the diesel fumes had rendered both stokers prostrate.

Such an alarming litany of shortcomings would have caused great consternation in SRD had things not suddenly begun to look up. The organisation, which had for so long struggled to carry out operations with unreliable and unsuitable craft, was now overwhelmed with good news.

At long last, special operations had access to a fully operational fleet. *Tiger Snake* and *River Snake* had been joined by their sister ships *Diamond Snake*, *Grass Snake* and *Sea Snake*; *Edouardo*, a vessel on loan from the Royal Navy, had finally been handed over; four fast-surface vessels were now in service, including *Karinya*, which had eventually arrived from Brisbane; *Taipan*, formerly a Chinese junk named *Bandoeng*, was soon to be commissioned; while two large 300 tonne vessels, *Mother Snake* and *Anaconda*, were already operating as mother ships to a small fleet of work boats and fast-surface vessels which the army and navy had recently made available. Such was the vast improvement in its fortunes that, ten days after *Krait*'s return from Timor, SRD was able to boast that it had the grand total of twenty-four craft in service and another nine, including two more Country Craft, either allocated or under construction.

On 1 August 1945, after almost three years of battling against insurmountable obstacles and incurring an expenditure running close to one million pounds, SRD announced that it was in a position to achieve its potential.

Fourteen days later, the war ended.

CHAPTER NINE

A Decline in Fortune

After years of bitter warfare, the sudden cessation of hostilities with Japan took everyone, including SRD and the Lugger Maintenance Section, by surprise. Special operations were cancelled or, in the case of Crocodile party, which had only reached the stage of carrying out its preliminary reconnaissance, aborted. Others were diverted to more peaceable roles. One of these, Semut IV, had been awaiting insertion into Sarawak to suss out pockets of Japanese, who had gone to ground when the Australian 9th Division had arrived to retake Borneo in July. With the whole of North Borneo in administrative chaos after years of Japanese occupation, it was decided that all Semut operatives could make themselves useful by temporarily assuming civil control of many areas until the British Borneo Civil Administration (BBCAU) could take over. It was also decided, with SRD's headquarters long since transferred to Morotai, the Darwin base closing down on September 5 and the entire organisation ordered to be dissolved by the end of October, that the time had come to dispose of SRD's newly acquired but now very redundant fleet.

Such was the haste with which Special Operations wished to shut up shop that on 22 August 1945, a mere eight days after the war ended and before GHQ even had time to work out the surrender plan, a meeting was called in Borneo to discuss the disposal of all the equipment and material belonging to AIB, SRD and FELO. At this meeting, attended by high-ranking members of all three organisations, it was resolved that the best way to unburden themselves of surplus material, which included SRD's fleet, was to recommend its transfer to BBCAU. Since some of the vessels had already arrived at Morotai and the rest, including *Krait*, were due to sail from Darwin that very day, this proved to be a popular solution.

No one was more pleased to learn of this plan than Darwin's Naval Officer in Command, who was delighted to be rid of *Krait*. Yet another disparaging report had declared the ship completely useless for naval operations — an opinion that had oft been voiced by various personnel since 1944. Not only was she considered to be unfit for duty, but it had also been discovered (with no upgrading in the sanitation department since Jaywick), that the officers had to use the same 'head' as the men — a situation the Senior Service considered to be most undesirable. Such was the Navy's relief to be rid of a vessel which it now considered to be a distinct liability that instructions were issued to tow her to Morotai if necessary. To absolve itself of any responsibility should anything untoward occur during the voyage, the Navy had also made sure that SRD was in no doubt as to the vessel's limitations.

Despite the Navy's misgivings, *Krait* made the week-long voyage to Morotai under the watchful eye of her corvette escort, HMAS *Gympie*, unaided and without mishap. At Morotai she passed into the control of the Naval Officer in Command of the Moluccas Islands and the following month was dispatched, by way of Halmahera Island and Celebes, to Ambon. Here, on September 22, in company with eleven other vessels, including HMA Corvettes *Glenelg*, *Cootamundra*, *Rockhampton*, *Junee* and *Latrobe*, and SRD craft *Anaconda* and *Nyanie*, she was present at the ceremony at which the Japanese in Ambon formally surrendered. With the exception of the now vanquished and very chastened Japanese, it was a joyous occasion, particularly for the local Ambonese children who swarmed onto *Krait*'s deck to share with her crew a case of delicious juicy apples — something they had not seen for some time, if at all.

Less than a fortnight later *Krait* was off on her last mission, having spent the intervening period providing transport for investigation teams searching for fugitive war criminals and the graves of Allied servicemen. With thousands of small islands to re-occupy and with communication links almost non-existent, small Allied advance parties were also fanning out to establish whether the Japanese troops in the area had laid down their arms. Consequently, *Krait*, under the command of Harry Williams, sailed south-east from Ambon on October 4 to carry out a survey and a reconnaissance of Banda and then Aru Island, where she was to rendezvous with her old friend, HMAS *Gympie*.

Twenty-four hours later she arrived at her first destination. After receiving a warm welcome from the local population, the investigation team learned that although all the Japanese had fled, they had left behind a substantial stockpile of aviation fuel and a sizeable cache of aerial bombs, still in their cases, at the old fort. As soon as they had noted these details and photographed the grave of a lone RAAF pilot who had crashed his Kittyhawk on the island in December 1944, Williams weighed anchor and set a course for the village of Dobo, Aru Island, their next port of call.

They ran into trouble almost immediately. Although two additional ventilators had solved the problem of the foul air in the engine room, there had been no time before the ship left Darwin to modify the for'ard storage hatches, which had always allowed water to enter the hold in anything other than a calm sea. With huge seas running for almost the entire two-day journey to Aru, it was not long before the area below decks was awash, soaking the bedding, damaging the intricate survey equipment beyond repair and saturating the wireless, making communications with the outside world impossible.

However, when they arrived at Dobo, the discomfort of the journey was all but forgotten. Although the Japanese at the small garrison were unprepared for *Krait*'s arrival they soon made up for it, telephoning their headquarters at Dokub Bara, down the coast on the Serwatu River, and giving the visitors a cordial welcome. The following day, leaving Williams in charge of *Krait*, which was unable to navigate the shallow Serwatu, Lieutenant Chapman (RANVR) and five of *Krait*'s ten-man party left for Dokub Bara, a nine-hour barge journey from Dobo. On their arrival, and much to their astonishment, they found a large number of Japanese, including members of the crack Imperial Japanese Guards Regiment — the conquerors of Singapore, no less — ready and waiting for a full ceremonial surrender. With all due solemnity, the Australians accepted the officers' swords and other paraphernalia, rendered the field guns inoperative and inspected the vast ammunition dumps. It was not until decades later, when he had heard that some of *Krait*'s former members had been beheaded in Singapore following the Rimau raid, that Lieutenant Chapman realised how ironic this unexpected surrender to a handful of the ship's present crew had been.

With the formalities over, the six-man party set off the next morning on a two-hour journey downstream to rendezvous with *Krait* at the mouth of the river, only to find no sign of her. A report from one of the locals that a large and fiery explosion had been observed out to sea did nothing to allay their anxiety. The party made its way back up the coast by barge to an alternate emergency rendezvous at Dobo, wondering, since Japanese communications to Ambon were hit and miss, how long it would be before they were rescued. Fortunately, the following day, October 10, they were reunited with *Krait*, having spent a very uneasy night in the Dobo garrison camp. Their nervousness did not stem from the proximity of the Japanese, who were most anxious to be circumspect at all times, but from the unrest among the local population whose feuding Moslem and Christian factions did not see eye to eye.

On October 13, HMAS *Gympie* arrived, carrying troops who were to assume responsibility for the post-surrender organisation and to take charge of the mountain of goods *Krait*'s team had collected from the Japanese. However, it was not until the following night, when the ship's waterlogged radio eventually dried out enough to permit transmissions, that Ambon learned of the spectacular surrender ceremony which Chapman and his small band had been privileged to witness.

By the time *Krait* returned to Ambon on October 18, the final details of her future, and the future of the other SRD craft, had been decided. As soon as practicable, all vessels would definitely become the property of BBCAU. This news was indeed welcome to both the British Borneo Administration and the Australian 9th Division. With only three workboats and two slightly larger vessels at its disposal, BBCAU had been forced to rely on water transport belonging to the AIF, which had

While citizens pass by oblivious, grief-stricken Chinese women mourn the loss of a child killed by the bombing, Singapore City, February 1942.
Photograph Australian War Memorial, Canberra (AWM 11529/22).

Captain William Roy Reynolds, Master Mariner.

Taken immediately before her arrest on 8 December 1941, this photograph of *Kofuku Maru*'s sister ship, *Fukuyu Maru*, shows the similarity between the two vessels and the method of registration.

Lieutenant-Colonel Albert (Bertie) Coates, to whom Reynolds delivered the injured castaways.

Ivan Lyon of the Gordon Highlanders.

Commando training, Refuge Bay, late 1942.

Lyon and his fellow escapees on board *Sederhana Djohanes*, March 1942.

Jaywick Originals 1942, Refuge Bay. Taken on the road to nearby West Head.
(Back row) Happy Huston, Morrie Wright, Fred (Boof) Marsh, Tiny Hage, John Mackay.
(Front row) Joe Jones, Snow Kerr, Stan McCabe, Mick Cameron.

Boof Marsh and Tiny Hage paddle HMAS *Lyon* out to greet *Krait* at Refuge Bay, 17 January 1943.

Krait at anchor, Refuge Bay, 17 January 1943.

Ivan Lyon (rear) with Happy Huston, Cobber Cain and Horrie Young left to right) at Exmouth Gulf, September 1943.

Subar Island, the observation post for the Jaywick raid.

Nasusan Maru. Although seven ships were blown up on the morning of 27 September 1943, the Japanese managed to salvage all but two. *Nasusan Maru* and one other were so badly damaged that they sank.

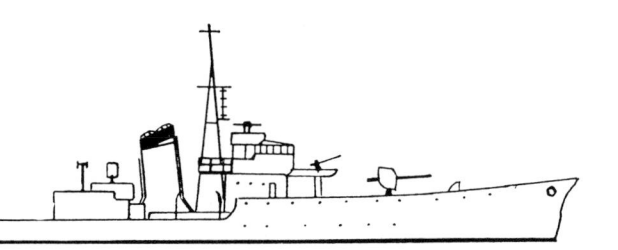

Sketch of Japanese minesweeper No 17, identified by Donald Davidson as being very similar to the patrol boat that paced *Krait* in the Lombok Strait, 11 October 1943.

Taken at Meigunyah, Brisbane, after its return from Operation Jaywick, the final Jaywick team with Jock Campbell of SRD.
(Back row) Moss Berryman, Boof Marsh, Joe Jones and Happy Huston.
(Centre) Crilly the Cook, Cobber Cain, Paddy McDowell, Horrie Young, Poppa Falls, Taffy Morris.
(Front row) Ted Carse, Donald Davidson, Ivan Lyon, Jock Campbell, Bob Page.

HMAS *Tiger Snake* photographed for posterity, after her arrival in Darwin, 5 February 1945.

On 6 June 1945, only 2 months before the war ended, guns were fitted to *Krait*'s decks.

Part of the Rikki Tai's Guben prison, Surabaya, in which Reynolds was incarcerated until his execution, 8 August 1944. Photograph taken Anzac Day 1991.

Part of the doorjamb of the cell in Balikpapan, Borneo, upon which Bill Reynolds scratched details of his imprisonment, November 1943-February 1944.

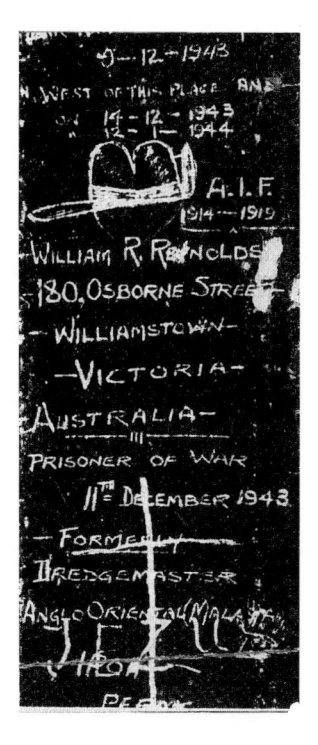

Bessie Reynolds as a young woman.

Resplendent in her new paintwork, *Krait* is lowered from the deck of P&O's *Nellore* into the Brisbane River, following her purchase from River Estates, Borneo, April 1964.

Watched by Fred (Boof) Marsh's childhood friend, Sylvia Crane, and Ted Carse, far right, Mrs Ivy Marsh smashes the champagne bottle across the bows as she renames the ship MV *Krait*.
Photograph The *Courier Mail*, Brisbane.

Krait as a coastal patroller on Sydney Harbour.

Krait's master, Bill Cockbill, of the Volunteer Coastal Patrol, takes a sight while on patrol duty.

Krait as refugee boat *Tuong Lei* in the ABC television series 'Patrol Boat', 1978.

Death of a hero?

Will this be your sentence to one of Australia's greatest wartime veterans?

In the spring of 1943, a marine raid was fired into Japanese-held territory from secret headquarters in Australia.

The men, from the highly trained Z-Force.

The ship – 'Krait'.

Her mission, to destroy enemy shipping in Singapore Harbour.

"Operation Jaywick", the first and perhaps the greatest Australian sea raid of World War II was the brain-child of Major Ivan Lyon of Z-Force.

An extraordinary raid which epitomised the particular brand of brave eccentric Australian courage.

For 47 days, 33 of which this 80 ton 'Krait,' flying a Japanese flag for camouflage, carried her 14 man crew deep into enemy-held waters.

Nearly two thousand miles from their base and far beyond all hope of rescue.

Together, crew and ship steamed over 5,000 miles of Japanese occupied sea to finally drop anchor on September 18, within 30 miles of the heavily defended Singapore Harbour.

There, 6 men in three canoes armed only with magnetic explosive limpets, a supply of food and a case of cyanide tablets, left the relative security of 'Krait' to paddle the thirty miles into Singapore Harbour.

'Krait' then moved on. An aimless steaming, 1500 miles off the islands of Borneo. Aware of the danger of attracting attention if she stayed in one place too long.

A dangerous two week wait for the appointed rendezvous date.

A rendezvous which she met not knowing if the raid on Singapore Harbour had been a success or if she was in fact sailing into a trap.

The rest is history.

As 'Krait' picked up her raiders, and as Japanese fighters searched overhead for her, news broke around the world of the destruction of over 40,000 tons of Japanese shipping.

Japanese defence forces in Singapore were in chaos.

"Operation Jaywick" was home.

No single action of World War II stands out as a true example of enterprise and courage than this daring and completely successful raid made by the handful of men from Z-Force and of the heroic action of the tiny 80 ton motor vessel 'Krait'.

A mission of such imagination and bravery that even the Japanese called them heroes.

Every man who took part in the raid was decorated.

But what of the 'Krait'?

What of the hero who was not only instrumental in the success of "Operation Jaywick", but in many other dangerous missions during World War II.

'Krait', part of our Australian heritage is in more danger today than she faced during all the battles of the war.

The danger – Neglect.

This Australian hero is under threat of being lost to the Nation forever, unless enough money can be raised to save her.

Her hull is rotting. She is in desperate need of repair and restoration.

We need your help.

The Krait Appeal Fund has set its target at $250,000. But we need much more if we are to restore and save this great Australian for posterity.

Restored to carry on her peacetime role, not just as a museum piece, but as a living reminder of the Nation's debt to servicemen and women.

'Krait' is a symbol of self-sacrifice and a token of Australia's heritage.

Your contribution is vital to her survival.

Don't let her wartime achievements be forgotten.

Don't sentence this National hero into obscurity.

This gallant little ship deserves more. Give her a future.

Help save the 'Krait'.

Send your donations to The Krait Appeal Fund, Box 1984, G.P.O., Sydney.

The Krait Appeal.

In 1981, with the aid of posters such as this, 'The Krait Appeal' raised more than $220,000.

Krait crosses the Ballina bar on her way for a refit, 4 February 1981. Photograph *The Northern Star*, Lismore.

Work begins to make *Krait* seaworthy, Ballina, 1981.

Before.

After.

Before and after. *Krait*'s single hatch is replaced by four small hatches, along with new decking, Ballina, 1981.

Model of *Krait* made by Wayne Masters from the drawings of Sid O'Dwyer, Australian War Memorial, Canberra.

The War Memorial in Surabaya, Java, where Major Tom Hall held his 1991 Anzac Day dawn service for Bill Reynolds and other Allied personnel executed by the Japanese.

Krait being returned to her wartime appearance by the Australian National Maritime Museum, July 1991.

Author Lynette Ramsay Silver and Major Tom Hall photographed on *Krait* in September 1991.

resulted in protests from the military that civil matters were tying up vessels needed to transport urgent supplies to troops.

With the handover of SRD vessels to BBCAU due to take place on November 2, *Krait* left Ambon for Labuan Island, on Borneo's west coast, shortly after her return from Aru. It was fitting that on this, her last voyage, she would return to the same waters through which she had passed on her journey to Singapore for Operation Jaywick and in which she had undertaken her aimless wandering, a little more than two years before.

All went well until the ship neared the coast of south-west Borneo. In what appears to be an acute case of deja vu, the ship's navigator lost his bearings in a severe storm, headed in the dark for the shoreline instead of the open sea and, in almost the same place that Ted Carse had run the ship aground in September 1943, very nearly lost her.

Except that the crew's lives were in obvious jeopardy, it might have been better for all concerned had she foundered. At the eleventh hour, it had been revealed that *Krait*'s ownership was in very serious doubt.

Although the Admiralty, the Australian Naval Board and SRD had known that Reynolds's salvage claim had been awaiting attention for the best part of two years, it had hit such a minefield of red tape that it had never been resolved. While everyone from Lord Louis Mountbatten to the Naval and Army chiefs had been quick to realise *Krait*'s potential in 1942 and had embraced the victorious return of the Jaywick team with patriotic fervour, no one, it seemed, in either Britain or Australia, wanted to become involved in a complex administrative and legal wrangle.

Since Great Britain was responsible for its colonial outpost of Singapore, Reynolds had, in 1943, referred his claim to the Colonial Office London — the agency whom he and his solicitors believed would be best equipped to deal with it. After more than twelve months' delay, the Colonial Office, at a loss how to cope with the problem, referred it to the Admiralty. The Admiralty, guessing quite rightly that the Australian Naval Board would not want to assume responsibility, was forced to address the issue and asked the Department of Naval Intelligence for information regarding *Krait*'s previous ownership.

Therein lay the problem. Information, other than that which Reynolds had supplied regarding his takeover of the vessel, was scant. With hostilities preventing any investigation of her Japanese ownership until the war was over, the only concrete fact to emerge was that *Krait*, then known as *Kofuku Maru*, had been taken into custody on 8 December 1941 and had become the responsibility of the Custodian of Enemy Property, Singapore. Since the international rules of war regarding seizure of property are very strict, requiring all confiscated goods and objects to be returned to their rightful owners once hostilities have ceased, this revelation confused the matter even further.

Although at the time the Colonial Office undoubtedly had paperwork from Singapore that would have shed light on the issue, particularly since Dickie Dickinson had kept tabs on all registered Japanese vessels for a considerable period before the war, it was not consulted. Paranoiac about keeping the very existence of SRD, let alone its activities, a secret from everyone including the Colonial Office, the Department of Naval Intelligence instituted a total security clampdown.

On 22 February 1945, the Admiralty was advised that although Reynolds might have difficulty proceeding with his claim against an individual or a government body, he appeared to have a perfectly valid claim to recover his salvage reward against the ship herself. However, because of the security angle, this legal opinion was not passed on to the Colonial Office. With the right hand not knowing what the left hand was doing, the Colonial Office, in order to rid itself of a matter in which it did not wish to be involved, decided to refer Reynolds's claim to the Australian Naval Board. Since the Board had already told the Admiralty that it disclaimed responsibility, Reynolds's claim was now on the bureaucratic merry-go-round.

In an effort to be free of what was becoming a nightmare of buck-passing, Australia's Naval Board Liaison officer in London suggested that the entire file should be passed to the head of SRD. There the matter would have remained, pushed aside in SRD's 'too-hard-basket' had it not been decided to transfer *Krait* to BBCAU.

With everyone, from General Blamey down, anxious to eliminate any trace of SRD and its activities by the end of October,

A Decline in Fortune

it must have come as a considerable shock to discover that the organisation had never in fact had any right to the vessel. She had never been purchased, neither had she been requisitioned. In short, SRD had outfitted, maintained and used a vessel for which it had no legal right and for which it had not one scrap of paperwork.

Unable to resolve the situation by November 2, the handover date for the rest of the craft, SRD sought frantically for an answer to its predicament. It was finally decided that the responsibility for *Krait*, since she had come into SRD's hands via Ivan Lyon and SOE, was definitely a matter for the British element of SRD.

In what was an inspired piece of additional lateral thinking, SRD Headquarters also suggested that if any further information was required that application should be made to Force 136, India. Since this was the still highly secret Far East component of SOE which had given Jaywick the go-ahead and which, like SRD, did not officially exist, SRD had neatly extricated itself from a very embarrassing situation.

While this transfer of responsibility was a clever solution to the problem, it did not solve the pressing question of *Krait*'s disposal, which had become further complicated when BBCAU announced that it did not want her after all. It was no use arranging for her to have an accident or scuttle her, since the question of compensation for her loss would instantly arise.

In what appears to be another brilliant flash of inspiration it was decided the best thing was to come clean and confess that there was an outstanding salvage claim on the vessel, whose ownership would have to be decided through a Prize Court in Singapore. Because SRD had now decreed that the British were ultimately responsible for *Krait*'s future, it was also decided that the best solution would be to hand her over to an organisation known as 50 Civil Administration Unit which, being a purely British component of BBCAU itself, would satisfy the criteria. 50 CAU's Brigadier McCaskie (Chief Judge and Deputy Governor of North Borneo, and Chief of BBCAU) was willing to accept the ship on the condition that she must be returned to Singapore for a Prize Court hearing; he also undertook to ensure that she was properly disposed of when the time came. These requirements having been established, *Krait* was paid off in Labuan on 12 December 1945.

Her transfer to Brigadier McCaskie and 50 CAU was a load off everyone's mind. SRD had rid itself of a tremendous liability, the Admiralty had salved its conscience by gaining answers to its questions and 50 CAU had the use of a vessel until such time as the salvage claim came to court.

That it did not is an indictment upon the British judicial system and a triumph for civil servants who would much prefer that such matters were never brought before the public gaze. Although the file remained open and it was well established that *Krait*'s ownership was in very great doubt, no moves were made to uncover the identity of her original Japanese owner, from whom the vessel had been confiscated on 8 December 1941, nor did anyone make any move whatsoever to deal with Reynolds's valid claim for salvage. Lost in a maze of red tape by bureaucrats who had no interest in resolving the matter, the ownership of *Kofuku Maru* was destined to remain in limbo indefinitely.

There was no chance that Reynolds would activate the file, for by December 1945 he was dead. At Surabaya, Java, less than fifteen hundred kilometres from where *Krait* rode at anchor at Labuan, all that remained of William Roy Reynolds were the charred fragments of a few bones scattered about the sand of the desolate Eastern Fort.

CHAPTER TEN

A Forgotten Hero

When Bill Reynolds had volunteered to become part of the highly secret Bureau of Economic Warfare in 1943, he had entered a world far more dangerous than that of any other secret organisation. While SRD was undoubtedly a highly irregular outfit, many of its missions paled into insignificance when compared to those undertaken by civilians attached to the Bureau. It was for this very reason that Reynolds and all those who elected to volunteer for such perilous work were paid vast sums of money — in cash.

Once the Bureau had learned that Reynolds was fluent in Malay, had a good working knowledge of Chinese and knew the waters of South East Asia as intimately as his own backyard, it had wasted no time in making use of his talents. In November 1943, at about the same time that his young friend Ivan Lyon was in Brisbane toasting Jaywick's success, Reynolds was heading north from Australia along the very same route followed by *Krait* only weeks before. Unaware that his old fishing boat had ever left Cairns, let alone carried the Jaywick raiders to such dizzying heights of victory, Bill Reynolds had entered a world which to him was completely alien.

Gone was the invigorating tang of the salt-laden air, along with the rhythmical thud of waves smacking against *Krait*'s rough wooden hull. Gone, too, was the shimmering line beyond the narrow bow where sky and ocean merged into a pale and distant horizon. In their place were the claustrophobic atmosphere of warm recycled air, the almost indistinguishable purr of far-off diesel engines and clammy, confining walls of iron that ran with constant streams of condensation. After a lifetime of running before the wind, Captain William Roy Reynolds, Master Mariner, had become Mr W. R. Reynolds, secret agent and submariner.

Safe and anonymous beneath the surface, the American submarine USS *Tuna* encountered none of *Krait*'s hazards as she cut through the waters of the Lombok Strait and entered the Java Sea. Leaving the towering volcanoes on Bali and Lombok behind she did not head west towards Java, as *Krait* had done, but held her course to the north. When she reached the entrance to the Macassar Straits she stopped and surfaced. Out in the tropical darkness, about three kilometres to the west, was Laut Island — Reynolds's destination.

In the guise of procuring a junk loaded with quinine and rubber for black-market operations, Reynolds's mission was to make contact with Chinese secret agents who were operating in the area. Once he had obtained vital intelligence and information, for which vast amounts of money had been placed at his disposal, he was to make his way back to Exmouth Gulf in the trading vessel. The fact that he was to carry out this highly risky mission alone did not worry Reynolds, who evidently considered such a task to be no more dangerous than any other he had undertaken since the calamitous fall of Singapore. At twenty past ten on the night of November 14 a handful of admiring and incredulous American submariners had watched the lone Australian, who at fifty-one years of age was older than many of their fathers, step into his small rowing boat and paddle away into the night with nary a backward glance. Three days later he was in Japanese hands.

When Reynolds was captured at the village of Kota Bahru, after being betrayed to the Japanese by local natives, he was taken 270 kilometres north of Laut to the mainland town of Balikpapan, Dutch Borneo, where he was imprisoned in Sentosa Barracks, a small building that had been converted to a gaol. During the next three months, realising that his prospects were not altogether bright, Reynolds had carefully and methodically scratched into the wooden door jamb of his cell his personal details as well as a sketch of a slouch hat — evidently in the hope that this easily recognised symbol might alert someone at a later date that he was an Australian. His last entry was made on 10 February 1944 when, in rather chilling contrast to his usually meticulously

A Forgotten Hero

neat printing, he had hastily scrawled a message that he was being taken to Surabaya, Java.´

A worse place to be imprisoned would have been hard to find. Under peace-time conditions Surabaya was hardly inviting. Under Japanese occupation it was less so. Based in the town — which was no more than a ramshackle collection of decaying Dutch colonial buildings and poorly kept native dwellings surrounded by rice paddies — were some of the most barbaric officers serving in the Imperial Japanese Forces. Torturing prisoners, irrespective of race, was a way of life. Trials for Europeans were non-existent and, as soon as the cells looked like becoming overcrowded, the Japanese had devised a most efficient method of clearing them — executing the prisoners.

It was to this hell hole of suffering and bloody excesses that Bill Reynolds was taken. He was handed over on his arrival to the Rikki Tai, or Land Garrison Unit, which conducted its unsavoury business at 116 and 118 Sumatrastraat. For six months, apart from a sojourn to the stockade for questioning from May until June, Reynolds was kept in the Guben prison cell block, where, because of his ability to speak Malay, he wasn't allowed contact with any other person, Indonesian or European. So fluent was his command of the language that some of the Japanese guards believed he was of mixed race.

On 8 August 1944, the Japanese commander decided that the time had come to dispose of the current batch of prisoners, including Reynolds and a number of Indonesians who had been charged with stealing telegraph wire from the store at the Eastern Fort and from the nearby Naval Garrison Unit. At eight that morning, without any fanfare, and without any trial whatsoever, Reynolds was hustled out of his cell and bundled into a truck with the Indonesians. Half an hour later they, and a second truck carrying a detachment of guards, arrived at the execution ground — a stretch of wasteland about two hundred metres from the Eastern Fort of the harbour, which the Japanese had renamed the Higashiguchi Battery.

Upon arrival at the Fort, the prisoners, who were handcuffed and blindfolded, squatted down in front of a hut to wait. Shortly afterwards three more Europeans, also handcuffed and blindfolded, arrived from the stockade, accompanied by an interpreter and three guards. Since executions aroused a great deal of interest, despite their frequency, there was quite a sizeable gallery. Included in the fifty or so onlookers were Lieutenant Yoshimoto, who had given the order to execute the prisoners; his assistant Ensign Okada, one of those who had accompanied Reynolds to the Fort; the legal officer representing the court which had sentenced the Indonesians; the interpreter Senuma; Warrant Officer Ikeda; five armed soldiers; officers from the Surabaya Naval Base and a hotchpotch collection of officers, NCOs and ordinary troops who were passing through Surabaya and who had decided to drop in to view the proceedings. To one side of the audience, ready and waiting, was a freshly dug pit about two metres wide and two metres deep.

After interpreter Senuma had read the death sentence to the victims in Malay, all but one of those who understood the language had been reduced by shock to a state of near collapse. Numbed with terror, the first group of Indonesians kneeled meekly beside the pit while eager volunteers from the army rank and file cut off their heads.

With rank amateurs volunteering for the task, it was neither a clean nor a swift execution. The executioner assigned to the third or fourth prisoner botched the job completely, leaving his victim alive and only partially decapitated. Exceedingly annoyed by this display of outrageously inept swordmanship, Lieutenant Yoshimoto ordered Yamashita, a clerk attached to the Naval Unit, to finish off the prisoner with a spear that was resting against the wall of the hut. His hand trembling uncontrollably, Yamashita failed miserably at his first attempt and succeeded only in inflicting a wound below the left shoulder blade. Forced to continue despite his obvious distaste for the job, Yamashita eventually managed to deliver the coup de grace by spearing the unfortunate victim through the heart.

Scared witless by the prolonged nature of the executions and the hideous attempts to spear their comrade, the three remaining Indonesians were now incapable of either standing or squatting. Unable to carry out the beheadings without reducing the already shocking proceedings to an even more bizarre spectacle, the Japanese were forced to shoot them where they had collapsed.

A Forgotten Hero

This left the three Europeans from the stockade and finally Bill Reynolds, whose subsequent act of defiance would be long remembered by the assembled Japanese. If the executioners for one moment expected that Reynolds would assist them in carrying out their grizzly task, they were in for a rude shock. Dressed in tattered pants and a shirt, his grey beard long from his lengthy confinement, the tall Australian stood rigidly at attention, his iron-rod bearing making it abundantly clear to all that he, uncowed and unbroken, was not going to accommodate the enemy. With all eyes of the now very interested gallery upon him, Lieutenant Yoshimoto was forced to re-assess the situation.

Clearly, here was a man who would not concede an inch — a prisoner who, even in the face of death, was so iron-willed and fearless that he would never bend before his captors, who, when standing erect, scarcely reached his chest. Mindful that the bungled execution had been responsible for a mortifying loss of face, Yoshimoto called a detachment of six guards aside and issued fresh orders. A few minutes later they formed a line, raised their rifles and took aim. Alone on that open killing ground, watched by an enemy which expected him to lose face by cracking completely at any second, the steadfast figure of William Roy Reynolds, MBE, now achieved final victory in death. Defiant and unyielding to the end, he crumpled only when the volley of shots forced the life from his body.

Heroic as Reynolds's last stand had been, five years would pass before anyone had any inkling of his fate and it would be another forty-six before the true circumstances of his death would be uncovered. Consequently, with Reynolds unable to agitate for the settlement of his salvage claim, the paperwork sat in the Admiralty office, in London. Back in Australia, Reynolds's wife, Bessie, knew only that her husband had not come home for Christmas 1943.

Had it not been for the official admission that Bill Reynolds was last seen paddling off to Laut Island on a mission known simply as 'Work Order No 14', she would not have known where he had disappeared. Although she canvassed the authorities for more information, none was forthcoming. It was not until May 1949, after a war crimes investigation team accidentally stumbled upon information about Reynolds while investigating the disappearance of two other Australians in Surabaya, that she was able to have him declared legally dead.

If Bessie expected that, in common with all other women whose husbands had died for their country, she would recieve a War Widows' Pension from a grateful government, she was to be bitterly disappointed. Being a civilian recruited by a very clandestine organisation to carry out secret espionage, Bill Reynolds simply did not officially exist. At an interview with the government minister concerned it was made abundantly and brutally clear to Bessie that, as there was no record of her husband's ever being in the armed services, she had no right to any remuneration whatsoever.

Left with virtually no income and with the bulk of the family assets lost during the battle for Malaya, Bessie, an independent and spirited woman, but one who had been comfortably off for most of her life, was forced to fend for herself. At a time when most working women of Bessie's age were thinking about retirement, the widow of one of Australia's finest heroes had to go out to work to make ends meet. Until the day she died she remained unaware that as Bill Reynolds's beneficiary, she had salvage rights to a ship which would have given her the financial security her husband had intended.

Despite the apathy of the British and Australian Governments, there *was* one person concerned about the outstanding salvage claim on *Krait*. This cautious individual was Mr R. B. Blade, Chief Secretary of North Borneo, who wrote to the Australian Army on 16 April 1947 requesting information about a ship named *Krait*, formerly *Kofuku Maru*, which had been taken over by the Marine Department of his administration in December 1945. As he noted there was an outstanding salvage claim in respect of the vessel, Mr Blade wanted to know how she had come to be in the hands of SRD and requested all details of her previous history.

His letter was one which the Army no doubt found impossible to answer, for it was not until Mr Blade sent a follow-up telegram on July 1 that anyone took any action. The Army's solution to his request for answers to some very tricky questions was simple. After a month's deliberation, it passed the buck to the Navy.

With SRD long since obliterated from the face of the earth, the Secretary for the Navy, Mr A. R. Nankervis, was obliged to answer the letter. The old file which contained the correspondence between the Admiralty and the Naval Board plus various bits of information given by SRD was located and an answer sent to Mr Blade. In his one page letter Nankervis gave a brief outline of the ship's history before neatly passing the buck back to Force 136, India. Since the files of Force 136 had, and still have, a top secret, one-hundred-year embargo on them until the year 2045, it is highly unlikely that even had he attempted to do so, Blade, who was simply a colonial civil servant, would have managed to obtain any further information.

As for the Admiralty, the question of *Krait*'s ownership was never raised again. Neither was it likely to be raised. Some years after the war, the entire file was destroyed.

Meanwhile, back in Borneo, *Krait* (now being used to deliver mail between Jesselton in the West and Sandakan in the east), had become a bit of a problem to Mr Blade's Marine Department, which wanted to get rid of her. Although the department had replaced *Krait*'s makeshift engine housing with a beautifully detailed timber structure, which was properly ventilated and very like the original, its marine personnel evidently had very little idea when it came to diesel engines. So poor was the maintenance that even the faithful Gardner could not cope with the neglect and more often than not *Krait* found herself tied up to the wharf at Labuan, her engine a mess.

It seems that *Krait*'s so-called unreliability was the major factor in the Marine Department's deciding to dispose of her. Whether or not Mr Blade was satisfied with the information that he had received from Australia about her previous history is not known. One thing is, however, beyond all doubt. In spite of Brigadier McCaskie's solemn undertaking to ensure that the ship reached a Prize Court in Singapore, she was put up for sale.

She was purchased by Mr R. G. Barrett of River Estates, a timber company based in Sandakan, on the east coast of Borneo, which required a work-horse to carry supplies to, and to tow lumber from timber camps on the Seganah River, to the south of Sandakan. Since *Krait*'s reputation for unreliability was well known, Mr Barrett acceded to the new crew's request to change her name to *Pedang* (Malay for 'sword' and one which was in keeping with other company vessels *Kriss*, a dagger, and *Sunpitar*, a blowpipe) in the hope that she might perform better. While it is odds on that it was proper maintenance that improved her performance rather than her new name, from that day on *Krait*'s engine never let her down.

Until 1963 the ship chugged along the waterways of northern Borneo, becoming slightly more tatty with each season. Although she more or less retained her original silhouette, her appearance changed in a number of ways to accommodate her new role in life. The for'head bulkheads were removed and the four small fish holds converted to one large area, into which crude bunks were installed for the crew members. To keep out the heavy monsoonal rain and the scorching tropical sun, a large awning that reached from the wheelhouse to the bow was also constructed. Her black hull was repainted white, as was her wheelhouse, but for all that, *Pedang* was still basically the same little vessel that Bill Reynolds had extricated from Singapore in those dark days of 1942.

By 1963 she had gone through a considerable amount of spare parts, including three propellers, which Gardners had supplied at regular intervals through their Far East agents. It is a tribute to British engineering that, despite a modicum of maintenance and some rather heavy-handed treatment, *Pedang*'s engine gave Mr Barrett no cause for complaint.

The ship would have perhaps lived our her days in genteel anonymity had two men on a flight out of Singapore in 1953 not engaged in a chance conversation. As a result of this discussion, *Krait*, instead of fading quietly into obscurity, was poised to enter the most turbulent period of her life.

CHAPTER ELEVEN

A Revival of Fortune

One of the passengers involved in the unexpected mid-flight encounter was Australian stockbroker Dick Greenish, a former member of SRD who was also, coincidentally, now the husband of Bob Page's widow, Roma. The other was an Englishman, a former maritime captain, who had been in charge of merchant shipping in Singapore. When the topic of conversation turned to the Jaywick raid, which by this time had been well publicised, Dick Greenish was astounded to learn from his companion that some years after the war *Krait* had been sold to a timber company which, he believed, operated in the Jesselton area of Borneo. He thought her name had been changed to *Pedang*.

Upon his return to Canberra, Greenish, who was naturally very interested in the matter for personal reasons, took every opportunity he could to uncover more facts about the whereabouts of the ship. Although *Krait*'s former crewmembers, Lieutenants Harry Williams and Bob Chapman, as well as Seaman Sid O'Dwyer, knew where she had been paid off and had harboured dreams of finding her again, their paths never crossed with that of Greenish.

For more than four years Greenish made no headway in his investigation until he met Mr M. Quinlivan, an Australian government official who was about to travel to Sarawak, Borneo, to establish a training programme under the auspices of an organisation known as the Colombo Plan. On learning about *Krait* and her wartime exploits, Mr Quinlivan promised to make enquiries in Sarawak.

Krait: The Fishing Boat That Went To War

All through the latter part of 1957 and into the month of January 1958, Quinlivan toured Sarawak extensively, asking about *Krait* at every opportunity but with no result. Then he arrived in Jesselton on January 30 to meet a Mr L. Jones for official discussions. In the course of their informal conversation Quinlivan asked Jones if he had ever heard of a ship named *Pedang*, alias *Krait*. To Quinlivan's surprise he replied that he had and volunteered the information that if anyone knew where she was, it would be the maritime authorities.

Within twenty-four hours Jones had the answer that Quinlivan had been longing to hear. *Pedang*, which was on the local maritime shipping register, was hauling logs at Sandakan, on the east coast. When this information reached an elated Dick Greenish the following month he began to take steps to bring *Krait* back to Australia.

It did not take long for the word to spread about Greenish's discovery, both in Australia and Borneo. Within days of learning that Mr Barrett could be persuaded to sell, contacts in Borneo had elicited from the North Borneo Government the promise that if the Australian government contributed half the cost of the purchase price of 6000 pounds, it would contribute the rest. While this may have been an attempt to make up for the civil administration's failing to ensure that *Krait* had reached the Prize Court as promised, the fact that her title was defective was unknown to Greenish, who saw the offer as a most magnanimous gesture. He realised also that the opportunity was too good to miss. With the support of ex-SRD members in the newly formed 'Z Special Unit Association, ACT', which wanted to help him bring *Krait* back and place her on display in Canberra, Greenish cabled Borneo that his organisation would guarantee to raise the 3000 pounds, if necessary.

Greenish knew that if he were to make his dream a reality he would need a great deal more muscle than that provided by a small group of returned ex-servicemen. Consequently, when Lord Louis Mountbatten visited Canberra in February 1961, a deputation headed by Greenish asked for his help. While Mountbatten was in no position to actively lobby the Australian government to provide funds for *Krait*'s return, he supported the idea in principle and, true to his word, wrote to naval chief Vice-

Admiral Sir Henry Burrell, on Greenish's behalf.

Sir Henry's reaction was disappointing, to say the least. He informed Greenish that he had investigated the matter and had come to the conclusion that the concept was not practicable. He did, however, suggest that both the Prime Minister and the Director of the Australian War Memorial would be amenable to displaying at the Memorial a suitable memento of *Krait*, or of the Jaywick raid, provided one could be found. This answer did not satisfy Greenish, nor his small band of followers, for by early 1962 he had learned that another Z Association was agitating for the return of the vessel — not just to Canberra but to the War Memorial itself.

On hearing in mid-1958 that *Krait* was in Borneo, Sydney based Dick Cardew, ex-SRD, had decided to drum up some interest. Working alone, he had first contacted One Commando Company at Sydney Harbour's Georges Heights. Being composed of fit, young and adventurous types, the Company was highly enthusiastic about the concept of returning *Krait* to Australia.

In August the following year, when Z Special Unit Association NSW was formed, Cardew was able to gain a little more clout. Although the Association had no funds at this stage to start a campaign to arouse support for his project, this worrying aspect was rectified the following month when Cardew, who often dropped in for a chat, again visited One Commando Company. On hearing that the fledgling Z Association was short of cash, Lieutenant Tom Hall decided that the least he and his colleagues could do was kick things along with some financial assistance.

At the upcoming Annual Commando Ball, in keeping with the finest traditions of the Australian Army, Hall (who had just embarked upon a private investigation into Operation Rimau) organised an illegal game of Two Up and handed Cardew one hundred pounds.

However, it was not until 1962 that Z NSW, which was working independently of the ACT faction, actively agitated to have *Krait* brought back and either placed in the War Memorial or handed over to One Commando Company as a training vessel. Despite the efforts of both lobby groups, neither one made any headway in their various demands. Dissatisfied with the answers coming out of Canberra, Greenish, with the support of his Z

Association and the ACT Advisory Council (of which he was a member), stepped up the campaign. For the whole of 1962 they dispatched a constant stream of letters to military chiefs, Ministers of the Crown, politicians, heads of ex-service organisations and even the Prime Minister himself. So did Z NSW.

Unfortunately, being bombarded with simultaneous demands for assistance from both Z Associations, the aims of each group became confused in the mind of the government, which began to provide stock answers irrespective of the original requests.

The entreaties by the Greenish faction for the government to put up the funds to purchase *Krait*, transport her to Canberra and house her in a suitable location fell on deaf ears, as did those of the NSW group. The government refused point blank to fund or support their proposals in any way. The Memorial (which had not been asked by Greenish to accommodate the ship) put it its two cents worth by declaring, quite rightly, that there was no space inside the Memorial building for such a large exhibit. It added that the vessel's present run-down state also precluded any possibility of her being either moored on the yet-to-be-completed Lake Burley Griffin as a floating exhibit or being housed outside in the Memorial grounds, where she would be exposed to vandalism, as well as the elements. In short, the last thing the Australian War Memorial wanted to inherit was a full-sized, aging and dilapidated wooden ship.

Neither did Greenish obtain any joy from the Returned Soldiers, Sailors and Airmen's League. Known universally as the RSL and one of the most powerful lobby groups in the nation, its National Secretary, Mr A. Keys, simply echoed the sentiments already expressed by the Memorial. Undaunted, Greenish tried a new tack, proposing that if she could not go to Canberra, the ship might be able to be used by the armed forces as a training vessel — a suggestion already raised by Z Association in NSW. The government was unmoved. Neither the Navy nor the Army was interested in taking on an out-of-date, hard-to-maintain, wooden ship for training purposes.

Despite the rebuffs, Greenish did not give up his campaign to bring the ship to Canberra, where he was convinced she belonged. Determined to counter the argument that *Krait* was a virtual wreck, he had her inspected by his SRD contact in

Borneo, police administrator John Walne, plus Mr A. D. Stevenson (the Sunlag party leader, who, despite having been stranded on Timor because of *Krait*'s failure to rescue him in 1945, had a soft spot for the vessel). Their glowing report that the ship was in A1 condition and was capable of being sailed to Australia cut no ice with the government, which stood by its original decision. It was not until extreme pressure was exerted by the ACT Advisory Council that the government eventually promised that when, and if, the vessel ever arrived in Canberra a site would be made available somewhere in the ACT.

With no funds to purchase so much as a nail for the ship, much less buy her and bring her to Canberra, the campaign may have fizzled out then and there had it not been for a groundswell of support from the Australian public. Despite official opposition, many ordinary Australians, particularly ex-servicemen, thought it a wonderful idea.

So did Alderman Harry Jensen, Lord Mayor of Sydney. The son of an ANZAC who had died at Gallipoli, he not only had close affiliations with One Commando Company, he was also politically astute enough to realise that *Krait*'s return was a potential vote winner. In June 1963, just ten days before Mr Barrett's offer expired and just as Z NSW was resigning itself that the best it could do was to negotiate for the purchase of *Krait*'s steering wheel, Jensen launched a public appeal through *The Sun* newspaper to raise 12 000 pounds — the amount that would be necessary to buy the ship and bring her back to Australia. Z NSW reacted almost immediately to Jensen's initiative by forming its own official fund-raising committee, headed by Major-General Denzil Macarthur-Onslow, Honorary Colonel of One Commando.

With so many prominent citizens involved in the project the campaign to buy *Krait* for the Australian people gained momentum. The Federal Government eventually made its contribution by deciding, since *Krait* was to be a 'floating war memorial' and open to public inspection, that all donations over one pound would be tax deductible. Luckily, since neither the armed services nor the War Memorial wanted her, the pressing problem of what to do with the ship when she arrived back in

Australia had been solved when the Volunteer Coastal Patrol, with which Macarthur-Onslow had connections, agreed to take her over for training and rescue purposes.

Although *The Sun* gave the appeal exceptional coverage, and the public responded enthusiastically, 12 000 pounds was a great deal of money — enough in 1963 to buy ten family sedans or two comfortable houses in suburban Sydney. Consequently, as Anzac Day 1964 — the date set for *Krait*'s arrival in Sydney — drew nearer, there was nowhere near enough money in the fund. The fact that the North Borneo Government had cut its contribution by half when it learned that the Australian Government had refused to advance any funds had not helped matters. Indeed, so desperate did the situation become that had it not been for donations of materials and goods from the business sector and the generous and timely donation of 3500 pounds from shipping tycoon Mr R. W. Miller, *Krait* would have remained in Borneo.

On 21 March 1964 Commander Harold Nobbs of the Volunteer Coastal Patrol arrived in Sandakan by air from Sydney to take over *Krait* and prepare her for the trip home. With only one month to go until Anzac Day, the original idea of sailing her to Sydney via Singapore, Java and Timor had long since been abandoned. Fortunately, the Eastern and Australian Line, a subsidiary of the shipping giant P&O, had agreed to ship her, free of charge, as deck cargo on SS *Nellore* as far as Brisbane, from where Nobbs and a volunteer crew, selected from hundreds who had applied, would sail her the last seven hundred-odd kilometres to Sydney. Harold Nobbs, a weather-beaten, burly little man who had served in the RAN as a lieutenant, was known for two things — his exceptionally fine seamanship and his inability to suffer fools gladly, just like Bill Reynolds. When he went to the slips at Sandakan to inspect the vessel he had travelled so far to see, he was appalled.

Krait was a picture of abject misery. Little more than a hulk, her hull was spongy with rot, her holds infested with vermin and her five-centimetre-thick planks sprung in a dozen or more places. To top it off, the sanitary arrangements were worse than ever and now consisted of nothing more than the hole in the deck, with a carved wooden foot socket on either side. Never

A Revival of Fortune

one to mince words, Nobbs declared her to be:

> '... indescribably filthy and neglected, her planking suspect, her engine in need of a complete overhaul ... The people in Sydney who assured us this ship held a Lloyd's certificate of seaworthiness are damned fools. Reputable shipping people here in Sandakan have appealed to me not to contemplate accepting *Krait* at any price. But I have told them I am acting on behalf of the people of Australia who have contributed so generously to establish this ship as a war memorial.
>
> 'I am not here to take delivery of a yacht, or even of a rough and ready workboat. I am buying a project — a symbol of the heroism of the men who manned *Krait*. If I can load her onto the deck of the freighter *Nellore* without breaking her back, and get her over the side again in Brisbane still in one piece, we'll cobble her up enough to get her to Sydney ... To make Sydney by Anzac Day we'll have to do in Brisbane a refit job that normally would take five months. So prepare the crew and as many volunteers as you can muster for a total effort — and don't lose your sense of humour!'

Five days after his arrival in Sandakan, as soon as he had established that the engine was in reasonable working order and had demolished *Krait*'s now derelict awnings, Nobbs handed over 4412 pounds (the equivalent of 30 000 Malay dollars) to become the custodian of what Mr Barrett described as 'one of his best ships'. The next day, after a tiring and difficult six-hour operation, *Krait* was lifted onto the deck of the freighter and firmly secured into a specially constructed cradle.

The next morning, while out to sea, the clean-up started. It was a herculean task. Before Nobbs and his helpers, recruited from *Nellore*'s crew, could even begin to start work they had first to eliminate the rats and cockroaches. When this was completed, they found that before they could remove the rotten ceilings and filthy bunks, no less than two tonnes of rubbish had to be shovelled out and dumped. Working sixteen hours a day and aided by hundreds of litres of disinfectant, detergent and paint, they had just enough time to get *Krait* into passable enough condition for her triumphant entrance into Brisbane on April 10.

The *Sun* had done its work well. There was hardly a citizen in the country who did not know that *Krait* had arrived back in Australia. For the ten days that the ship was at the Army Water Transport Workshops being repaired, refitted and recaulked and having her engine overhauled, there was a constant stream of visitors, from radio and television broadcasters to the Governor of Queensland. But of the hundreds who came to pay homage, or simply gawk at a vessel that many thought to be quite ugly, by far the most moved were the families of Jaywick's Andrew Huston and Freddie Marsh, both of whom had perished in Operation Rimau.

For Mrs Ivy Marsh, Fred's mother, the visit to the ship at her mooring on the Brisbane River early on the morning of Saturday April 18 was a very significant occasion. A pleasantly plump woman who was now getting on in years, she carried in her hand a bottle of champagne. The result of a bet between her son and Sylvia Crane, an old school friend, as to who would marry first, it had been won by Fred when Sylvia had taken the plunge while he was away on Operation Rimau. As Freddie had never returned to collect his winnings, the bottle had been kept, unopened, until this very special day.

Just before the ship, now resplendent in her new paint and canopy, and with her crew lined proudly on her deck, embarked upon her voyage to Sydney, Mrs Marsh smashed Freddie's bottle of champagne across the bows and officially renamed the vessel MV *Krait*. Escorted by a flotilla of small craft, *Krait* then headed out to sea.

By nine that evening, after being buffetted by gale force winds in Moreton Bay, *Krait* was leaking so badly that she was forced to return to Brisbane, where it was discovered that six planks were so rotten they would have to be replaced. Once more, shipwrights at the Army Water Transport Unit toiled ceaselessly to make her seaworthy and in the early hours of April 21, with a little over four days to go until Anzac Day, she left port again, only to be forced back by mountainous seas which threatened to swamp her at any moment.

A Revival of Fortune

Twenty-four hours later the seas had abated enough for Nobbs to try again. This time they were rewarded by a change in the weather which saw them steaming south under clear skies at a rate of an amazing eleven knots. *Krait* made such good progress that they reached Broken Bay with twenty-four hours to spare, allowing them time to visit Jaywick's old training camp at Refuge Bay and to carry out the late Paddy McDowell's dying wish to have his ashes scattered over the sea.

Under a cloudless blue sky the following afternoon, watched from the shores by a hundred thousand people and by millions on television, *Krait* made her way slowly up Sydney Harbour. On board were Jaywick veterans Jones, Carse and Young, who had made the voyage from Brisbane, and Moss Berryman who, having been spotted in the dockside crowd, had been whisked out by fast motor launch to join *Krait* as she came through the Heads. As a Scottish Pipe Band played 'Road to the Isles', one of Ivan Lyon's favourite tunes, the small ship left her escort of gaily dressed craft and entered Farm Cove, where she tied up at the Man o'War steps.

The reception from the thousands who had crowded the quayside to witness her arrival was tumultous. Standing before the assembled throng was an honour guard of soldiers from One Commando Company and the Governor of New South Wales, Sir Eric Woodward, who was representing the Governor General. Unfortunately, despite the media hype and the razzamatazz, there were some for whom this Vice Regal occasion was not quite so joyous as it appeared.

Due almost entirely to the publicity the vessel had received, *Krait* had by this stage achieved the status of a holy relic. Indeed, such was the shift of emphasis from the men who sailed in her to the ship herself that it was she, not they, who had become heroic. While a few individuals, who had viewed this trend with some disquiet, had been brave enough to voice their opinions, such unpopular sentiments had not been well received. Consequently, instead of being merely a tangible symbol, *Krait* had become an icon.

That the vessel had usurped the honours due to her Jaywick crew became abundantly clear as the time for *Krait*'s arrival at Farm Cove had neared. To their distress, the Jaywick relatives had been ushered without warning from their positions on the VIP pontoon moored beside the steps. Forced to jockey on the quayside for a position to view the proceedings, they had soon discovered why they had been moved. Their seats were required for people deemed to be more deserving — those who had been involved in some way in the ship's return, plus all those who wanted to bask in the reflected glory.

Pushed to one side, it was with mixed emotions that the families to whom *Krait* meant so much watched Sir Eric Woodward, in a short but moving ceremony, accept *Krait* as a war memorial on behalf of the Australian people. He then entrusted the vessel into the care and safekeeping of the Volunteer Coastal Patrol for use as a rescue and training vessel until such time as a suitable memorial site could be found. With the formalities and inspections over — the latter much to the relief of Nobbs, who in characteristic style deemed the crowds to be 'a nuisance' — *Krait* sailed off to her new career as a training and rescue vessel.

Unfortunately, since no one had bothered to lay down any proper guidelines, her passage was not destined to be upon smooth and untroubled waters.

CHAPTER TWELVE

Troubled Waters

Although the concept of a war memorial was very much at odds with *Krait*'s designated use as a working and training vessel, for the next nineteen years everyone, including the various members of *Krait* Fund Committee and Z NSW, was happy with the status quo. Except when it wanted Patrol members to crew the vessel for excursions, such as those organised for visiting Z Associations, or sail her to ports as far north as Cairns and as far south as Melbourne for Z reunions or special occasions, the Committee made few demands. Indeed, such was the relative lack of interest in the vessel that when funds dried up for her maintenance and day-to-day running, the Patrol was forced to cast about for alternative methods of income.

During the seventies in particular, when the *Krait* Committee's liabilities exceeded its assets and it was only saved from bankruptcy by a generous loan from one of the Committee's Coastal Patrol members, Nobbs and his successors Sandy MacKinnon and Bill Cockbill were forced to add fundraising to their other voluntary tasks. While there had been an emergency public appeal launched in 1971 to allow the Patrol to undertake urgent repairs, it had not been supported very well and the cost of the work, even with volunteer labour, had outstripped the amount raised.

Consequently, when Nobbs had discovered that a major overhaul of the engine was required in late 1973 it was fortunate that he was able to persuade several large firms to donate not only almost all the spare parts, thereby saving the Committee just on $4000, but specialised labour as well. With Patrol members putting in 2200 hours of unpaid labour, the entire job was carried out for a few hundred dollars.

Quite obviously, this hand-to-mouth existence was not at all satisfactory. In December 1974, with the Committee declaring that it was again considerably in the red and could no longer continue to assist in the financing of the vessel, things began to look rather grim. With no prospects of obtaining funds from any other source and realising that the public could not be expected to constantly dip into its pocket, the Patrol kept *Krait* afloat for the next two years by some innovative fundraising. Whenever interested groups asked to inspect and have an afternoon or morning out on the vessel, Skipper Sandy MacKinnon encouraged them to donate funds, which he then used for fuel and maintenance.

By this stage the *Krait* Committee, in an effort to rid itself of what was becoming a rather tedious responsibility, was taking active steps to move the ship to Canberra. However, to the Committee's consternation, it was made clear that even something as simple as a static outdoor display would require massive funds to prepare a site, construct a cradle and erect a suitable enclosure, not to mention the cost of transporting her from Sydney to the ACT. Since the government had no intention of providing the necessary funding, the Committee faced the daunting fact that if it intended to proceed with the project, it would have to raise the money itself.

The news that there were moves afoot to take the ship to the ACT was not greeted with joy by the Patrol, which was not at all anxious to part with the vessel. In 1977, determined to keep her seaworthy so that she would not turn into a museum piece, it formed a special *Krait* Division of its own. It was headed by the very energetic and outspoken Bill Cockbill, who had become *Krait*'s skipper.

An ex-sailor in the RAN, Cockbill resolved to find the wherewithall to save *Krait*, for which he had a great affection. Consequently, he stepped up the tours and inspections, pointing out to his visitors that, although the Patrol did its best to provide voluntary labour, a considerable sum was required if she were not to end up on blocks. The public was generous and by the time the visitors had given a donation, slipped their additional small change into a tin displayed prominently for that purpose, and purchased small mementoes, Cockbill had usually netted several hundred dollars.

From time to time, when the Patrol was asked to make *Krait* available for some festival or other, it readily agreed. Not only could it make the ship accessible for public inspection, which was part of its brief; Cockbill could also tout for donations to keep the ship running and build up the fund. Since these activities adequately paid for *Krait*'s not unsubstantial basic maintenance and running costs, the Patrol was able to continue to use the vessel to instruct groups such as Boy Scouts and Sea Cadets in the art of seamanship, to participate in rescue duties and to assist charities at fundraising activities — all without any cost to the recipients. The *Sun* newspaper, which had always given the vessel its utmost support, continued to play an active role by sponsoring the Patrol's Safe Boating courses.

By late 1979, due to the Patrol's untiring efforts, Cockbill's constant canvassing for donations-in-kind from the business sector, and a donation of $1500 from ABC TV to turn the ship into a Vietnamese fishing boat for an episode of *Patrol Boat*, the Committee had $4000 in the bank — far more than it had ever accumulated other than that raised by the public appeals made in 1963-4, and 71-72. With its financial state relatively healthy and the idea being bandied about to take *Krait* to Singapore in 1983 for the 40th Anniversary of the Jaywick raid, the Committee looked forward to an exciting new year.

However, time had now caught up with *Krait*. While engine repairs that were needed could be dealt with by resources available through the Patrol, major maintenance to the hull, which had been put off owing to the lack of necessary funds, could not. Cockbill announced that unless at least $100 000 could be raised, *Krait* would be unseaworthy within a year or two.

When requests for full funding from both State and Federal governments met with a negative response and with general donations looking most inadequate, Cockbill realised that unless something dramatic happened, *Krait* would be consigned to the scrap heap. Although it was hoped that the Committee's finances would receive a substantial shot in the arm from a film company that wanted to use the vessel for a movie, the amount anticipated was still a long way short of the target. With the Committee unmoved in any way to actively campaign for funds and the ship slowly deteriorating before his eyes, Cockbill had almost despaired for her future.

Then, in early 1981, just as he was wondering how the money could ever be raised, Bill Lovelock, executive producer of the highly popular television series *This is Your Life*, came to the rescue. Lovelock, an enthusiastic and energetic individual who had obtained permission the previous year to film an episode on *Krait*'s history for his programme, told Cockbill that the thing *Krait* needed was massive publicity. The best way to achieve it, he declared, was to first form a special fundraising committee of well known and influential people and then launch a massive appeal to coincide with the screening of *This is Your Life* on Anzac Day that year. It was figured that the sum of $250 000 should be sufficient to repair the ship, provide funds for ongoing maintenance and also have enough left over to take her on a re-enactment voyage to Singapore.

On 24 February 1981, with the help of such notables as Vice-Admiral Sir John Collins, a new group was formed under the patronage of well known Olympic yachtsman Sir William Northam. Its chairman was the dynamic Dick Mason, a former Royal Naval submariner and now Chief General Manager of Ampol, an oil company which had maintained an interest in *Krait* since 1964. Within weeks Mason and his team had organised the printing of very emotive posters and brochures, written dozens of letters to large corporations, prepared press releases and drummed up enough pre-publicity to ensure a wide viewing audience for *This is Your Life* on the night of April 25.

The television programme, followed by aggressive marketing, certainly did the trick. Money poured in from all over Australia from individuals, business houses and even the hitherto disinterested State and Federal governments, both of which contributed $25 000. Word even reached Mr Barrett and Gardner's in England, who sent substantial donations. So successful was the appeal that by the end of the year, with more than $130 000 raised, and with a tentative repair quote of $102 000 obtained from Ballina Slipway and Engineers on the NSW coast, Cockbill readied *Krait* for the long journey north.

She left Broken Bay on January 30. After a less than pleasant voyage, plagued by mechanical problems and battling seas so rough that the pumps were kept working overtime, she arrived at Ballina on February 2, only to discover that the conditions were too hazardous to cross the bar. Although the coast guard gave the all-clear two days later and sent a pilot on board, the seas were still far from favourable. After what must be described as a hair-raising ride through the breakers, *Krait* shot over the bar and into still waters, to the enthusiastic applause of several hundred well-wishers.

Within a week she was up on the slips and secured inside a special metal framework, where closer examination showed that the problems were far worse than anyone ever imagined. The repair and refit looked more like a five month job than the original estimate of five weeks. With costs escalating towards $170 000, the fund, whose name had been changed from *Krait* Appeal Fund to *Krait* Public Museum Fund to accommodate the new taxation laws, was kept open.

The shipwrights had barely made any inroads into their work when Mr Mason, the Musuem Fund Committee's chairman, dropped a clanger. At long last, and after many representations, the War Memorial had informed Z NSW that it was prepared to accommodate *Krait* provided that the costs of transportation to Canberra were met. Almost immediately after this announcement was made, a furore erupted, with angry letters appearing in the press from members of the public who claimed they had donated money to keep *Krait* in Sydney, in the water.

Unfortunately, they were right. Since the entire fundraising programme had been centred on the need to make the ship seaworthy, the public had been bombarded with statements extolling *Krait*'s value as a working ship. Painted as a 'hero' which should not be allowed to die, her good deeds had been listed in great detail and in such a way that there was no doubt in the mind of the general public that donations were imperative if she were to continue in this role. As there had never once been any suggestion during this period that she would go to Canberra, some sections of the public were understandably furious.

While the controversy raged, *Krait*, under the tender ministrations of the shipyard workers and the ever-watchful eye of the devoted Bill Cockbill, began to take shape. By the time she was released from her iron cage in the last week of August, she had undergone a transformation. Her rotten planks had been renewed, her stern rebuilt and her teakwood decks replaced with timber to the value of almost $30 000 — all of which had been generously donated by various Northern Rivers timber yards and sawmillers. She also looked a little more like the *Krait* which had taken the raiders to Singapore in 1943. Because the Memorial insisted that if the ship were to go to Canberra she must be returned as far as possible to her original wartime configuration, the large hatch had been replaced by four small ones.

Having emerged like a butterfly from a cocoon, it was now time to show her off. And what better place to start than the Commonwealth Games in Brisbane, where she would be seen not only by thousands of Queenslanders, but also by visitors from every Australian state and overseas. It was a proud moment for Bill Cockbill on 29 September 1982 when *Krait*, her flags flying jauntily in the breeze, led the procession of small craft escorting the Royal Yacht *Britannia* up the Brisbane River.

However, Cockbill's euphoria did not last for long. Under protest and against his better judgement, he handed the ship over to the Queensland Commando Association, which had been promised the use of the vessel for fundraising purposes by members of the *Krait* Committee. Although the Queenslanders, in the two months that they had charge of the vessel, raised $60 000 ($25 000 of which was donated by the Utah Foundation on the proviso that the ship be taken to Canberra), the unsuitable purposes for which *Krait* was allegedly used during this period raised the ire of some members of the public, thereby adding fuel to the already bitter debate about whether she would be better off in Canberra.

When Cockbill decided that it was time to go public, the controversy began to escalate, with the comments from opposing sides quite barbed at times. Some of the pro-Canberra faction, who had not been pleased to see the ship at either the start of the Sydney-Hobart Yacht Race or the Great Ferry Boat Race, now recalled that while *Krait* had been in the care of the Patrol she had often been seen ferrying people around the waterways — something that was now viewed with distinct distaste.

Although these were activities of which the Committee was fully aware, since a full Master's Report of *Krait*'s status and usage had been tabled at every meeting since 1964, there were rumblings of discontent that *Krait*, being a war memorial, should not have been used for anything other than passive activities. With no deeds of trust ever drawn up, no guidelines for the use of the vessel ever laid down and, indeed, not one skerrick of paper, other than the transcript of the handover ceremony in 1964, to indicate what was to be regarded as 'proper use', these protests were quite unfair. What the critics failed to realise was that had these fundraising excursions, suitable or otherwise, not taken place, *Krait* would have rotted and sunk at her moorings a long time ago.

There was no love lost either between Cockbill and the Queensland commandos, particularly when he had reported that on *Krait*'s return from Queensland at the end of 1982 she was minus a number of things, including a compass, navigational charts and Bill Reynolds's copper snake, which had been donated by his son on *Krait*'s arrival in Sydney in 1964 on the condition it remained with the ship. The commandos, for their part, demanded Cockbill's removal as Master of *Krait*, a position he still held, and intimated that unless this occurred they might be difficult about handing over the funds they had collected.

As if all this aggravation wasn't enough, the *Krait* Committee had discovered, rather late in the day, that although three of its members had been the nominal purchasers in 1964, the vessel did not belong to it, as had been assumed. Apart from the question of *Krait*'s defective title, which was evidently not known to them, the nominal purchasers had ceased to own the ship the day Sir Eric Woodward had accepted her for the Australian people who had, of course, put up the funds to buy her.

Neither, the *Krait* Committee learned, were the Trustees of the *Krait* Fund the Trustees of the vessel. That responsibility had passed to the Volunteer Coastal Patrol, to whom Sir Eric Woodward had entrusted her in 1964. As soon as this irregularity had been discovered in March 1981, the *Krait* Committee had called an emergency meeting and passed a resolution appointing

Jaywick telegraphist Horrie Young, Z NSW President John Gardner and Fund treasurer Ray Irish (who was also one of *Krait*'s original nominal purchasers) as Trustees to the vessel. However, recent legal advice had been received that these appointments may well be invalid, since evidently neither the *Krait* Committee nor Z NSW was authorised to make them.

Cockbill, who had obtained three separate legal opinions on the subject, pondered whether the Patrol members should mount a challenge and claim what his lawyers believed was theirs. In the end, he and his colleagues decided against it, figuring that to be a legally appointed trustee was to assume a most onerous responsibility.

From December 1982, when the ship returned from Queensland, *Krait* did not take on any extra public duties other than to carry out long-standing commitments which the Patrol felt duty-bound to fulfil. However, in his capacity as Master, since the Patrol's services were still required for maintenance and crewing, Cockbill continued to keep a watchful eye on *Krait*, which was now moored off HMAS *Penguin*, the Naval Depot at Balmoral Beach — the Committee having decided that the Patrol's mooring at Church Point was 'not secure'. Although access was difficult, since the vessel was tied up at a bouy, the Patrol was diligent in ensuring that the ship was checked regularly, and provided a crew when needed.

However, it was obvious that things could never be the same again. Apart from the fact that relations between Cockbill and the Committee were becoming more strained as times went on, the Taxation Commissioner, when granting the *Krait* Public Museum Fund its taxation concession, had imposed some rather stringent conditions. The one which affected the Patrol directly (now that there was a substantial amount left over from the appeal to maintain the vessel and fundraising was no longer needed) was that the ship had been given the status of a public museum and was not to generate income by taking paying passengers.

In the end, this ruling had little effect on Cockbill. In December 1983, he had had enough. Disillusioned and disappointed by the attitude of some of the Committee members after years of his unstinting and unselfish service, Cockbill resigned as Master of *Krait*.

Although the War Memorial had accepted financial responsibility for the vessel at the beginning of 1984, the Patrol actively continued to care for the ship while the debate about her future continued with no sign of a let-up. Petty jealousies arose, inflaming an already difficult situation and strengthening the resolve of all those who believed she should be entrusted to someone other than the Patrol. In 1985, after being kept in the interim period at her 'secure' mooring at Balmoral Beach, during which time the ship's bell disappeared, *Krait*'s future was eventually decided.

On April 22 that year she was formally handed over to the War Memorial, but, contrary to all previous announcements, she did not go to Canberra. As it had been decided to remove her from the care of the Patrol she was sent instead to Birkenhead Point, on the lower reaches of the Parramatta River, where the Sydney Maritime Museum was based. The Museum, which was composed almost entirely of enthusiastic voluntary workers with a passion for ships, was delighted to look after *Krait*.

Since it had been broadcast far and wide that she was to go to Canberra in December 1984, her removal to the Sydney Maritime Museum came as a surprise to many, particularly after all the kerfuffle that had taken place. Even while negotiations with the War Memorial had been under way the controversy had not waned. The Navy League, which supported *Krait*'s remaining in Sydney, had raised a petition, while politicians of all persuasions also added their voice to the protest.

Not unexpectedly, Bill Cockbill had refused to remain silent. While he conceded that *Krait* must one day come to the end of her useful life, he, in common with many others, believed that after all the expense and trouble that had been taken to get her into first-class shape, to place her in a museum at this stage was extremely premature. His outbursts had, naturally, aroused even more heated debate in the press, provoking Fund Trustee Horrie Young to attack all those whom he called 'Johnny-come-latelys'. Young, being Jaywick's telegraphist, had more right than most to voice his opinion. However, had Cockbill known at that stage that one of his most bitter opponents, Fund Trustee John Gardner (who was still President of Z NSW), had never belonged to either SRD or Z Special Unit, as he publicly claimed, he may have gained a moral, if not an actual, victory.

In the end, after all the hassles and bitterness, financial considerations won the day. After months of investigation by the War Memorial it was discovered that unless *Krait* was placed in a specially designed, humidity controlled exhibition building constructed especially for the purpose, she would dry out and simply fall to bits. As it was estimated that a building large enough to accommodate her, plus her transportation to Canberra, would cost in excess of 1.4 million dollars, the War Memorial had announced that it would be at least four or five years before it was in a position to take her. Until then, it decreed that she should be placed on public display and given adequate care to ensure that she did not deteriorate. In the meantime, those who did not live in Sydney would have to make do with a viewing of the scale model which the War Memorial had placed on display in Canberra.

And so *Krait* had come to Birkenhead Point. During the next couple of years she was placed on show and from time to time the Patrol, which was allowed access to her for Safe Boating Courses, was requested by the War Memorial and the *Krait* Committee to take visitors for short chugs around the harbour — an arrangement which did not altogether please the Sydney Maritime Museum, which, despite *Krait*'s being moored at its facilities, had no say in the movements of the vessel. In 1987, the War Memorial instructed the Museum to carry out several tasks, for which $47 000 was made available from *Krait*'s maintenance fund. Apart from minor maintenance, since the condition of the vessel was sound, the bulk of the funds appear to have been expended on removing all remaining fittings and fixtures installed by the Coastal Patrol which were now no longer needed and commissioning a set of plank expansion drawings, which gave the exact size and position of every single plank for future conservation purposes.

This work, a proportion of which was carried out by volunteer labour, had only just been completed in 1988 when the War Memorial dropped the bombshell. *Krait* would not be going to Canberra — ever. Instead, on December 2 that year, she would be transferred to the Australian National Maritime

Museum — a splendid building with extensive waterfront display facilities that was nearing completion at Sydney's Darling Harbour.

For the third time in as many years, *Krait* had a new custodian. Ironically, although the National Maritime Museum had a guaranteed source of income from the Federal Government, it did not need it for *Krait*. Fifty thousand dollars (the bulk of what remained of the 1981 fund) had been handed over with the ship to the Australian War Memorial in April 1985. Although the expenditure in 1987 had eaten substantially into the principal, it is the interest on the remainder of this publicly raised money which provides the funds to maintain the vessel.

In late 1991, when the Australian National Maritime Museum opened its doors to the public, *Krait* went on display. Although she was unencumbered by the fuel drums, supplies and all the other equipment that had crammed her holds and decks in 1943, it was the first time since her de-commissioning at Labuan in 1945 that she had come close to resembling the ship her Jaywick crewmen had known so well. Although in the almost sixty years that she has plied the waters of Far East Asia and Australia she has sailed under Japanese, Chinese, pseudo-Japanese, Australian and British colours, has been named sequentially *Kofuku Maru*, *Suey Sin Fah*, MV *Krait*, HMAS *Krait*, *Pedang* and MV *Krait* again, and has been, in turn, a Japanese fish carrier, an Allied rescue ship, a spy and relief vessel, a British Privateer, an escape craft, a special operations ship, a mail carrier, a log hauler, a supply boat, a training vessel, a Volunteer Coastal Patroller, a floating war memorial and a public museum, it is the Jaywick raid that has made her famous.

While the seven weeks that *Krait* spent on the Jaywick raid is but a speck in her long and varied history, it is a well known and well documented episode in her life and one that has captured the imagination of the public. Indeed, it was the only part of her past that had ever come close to being properly recorded. Although there abounded many colourful tales about her origins, her capture and her alleged post-Jaywick activities, there was little hard fact, making it difficult for those interested in her conservation to know where to start.

Hearsay, long accepted as being factual, had so distorted the real picture that it was not until 1990, when Major Tom Hall (the former army commando who ran the Two Up school to raise funds for *Krait*'s return to Australia) and I began a detailed investigation into her history that the real story began to emerge. Realising that *Krait*'s past was far more complex than any one had ever envisaged, we instituted a massive search to uncover the information that was required. While Major Hall travelled to London to comb the files of the Public Records Office, Admiralty, Foreign Office and various war museums and to interview people who had been intimately associated with the ship, I continued the laborious task of checking whether certain facts were indeed facts at all.

When Tom Hall returned from Britain in April 1991, having detoured to Surabaya on the way home to conduct a solitary Anzac Dawn Service in memory of Bill Reynolds and three other Australians who had died there as a result of Operation Rimau, we started to collate the thousands of pages of documents that had amassed.

To our amazement we found that, apart from the indisputable fact that *Krait* went on Operation Jaywick, almost every other statement ever made about her was either distorted or simply not true. Starting from scratch, we tracked down people such as Gardner's expert Bert Bevan-Davies, as well as Brenda Macduff and Marjorie de Malmanche, who had been rescued from Pompong by Reynolds, and stepped up our task of sifting through a mountain of private and public files for documents that would overturn the accepted version and establish the truth.

By the time we had finished, the stories about her origins, her capture, her pre-war role, her post-Jaywick activities and her post-war career had gone west. So, too, had the entertaining tale that while allegedly transporting the new Gardner engine to Cairns the undercarriage of a DC 3 aeroplane had collapsed on landing, so heavy was the machinery it was carrying.

Aided by the mass of new material we had unearthed and information obtained by researchers in Japan, plus the wealth

Troubled Waters

of evidence Major Hall had managed to uncover during his thirty-one years of research into Operations Jaywick and Rimau, we were able to clarify many points about *Krait* herself. Because of the close co-operation that exists between us and the Australian National Maritime Museum, we have been pleased to pass on this information to her engineers and conservators, enabling the Museum's dedicated staff to continue the lengthy and painstaking task of bringing her back to her Jaywick configuration. Although this work will take a number of years, such progress was made that towards the end of 1991 she began to look very much like the ship that Ivan Lyon had taken into enemy waters in September 1943.

Painted in her wartime colours, she is, like all those who sailed in her, unassuming, unpretentious but undeniably tough. Until such time as the question of her ownership, which has never been resolved, is settled, we, the citizens of Australia, remain her custodians.

As the visitors from all walks of life stream past her, she is many things to many people. For some she symbolises the outstanding daring and raw courage of Lyon and his raiders. For others she is a lasting and sacred memorial to all who perished in war, particularly those of her Jaywick crew who died on Operation Rimau. And for yet others she epitomises that exceptional bravery found in few men, one of whom was William Roy Reynolds, the man who brought her out of Singapore.

But no matter what she was or what she is, there is one thing she will always be: *Krait* — the fishing boat that went to war.

APPENDIX I

The Capture of *Kofuku Maru*: A Case of Mistaken Identity

In 1971, when *Krait* (alias *Kofuku Maru*) had become well known to many Australians, there appeared in the press a statement by a former RAN Petty Officer, Mr L. M. Sandy Boxsell, that the ship had been captured by the corvette HMAS *Goulburn* during a routine patrol of the waters near Singapore, shortly after the commencement of hostilities with Japan. The corvette's commanding officer, Basil Paul, who was interviewed in 1974 when *Krait* visited Melbourne, attested to this fact and before long this statement, along with the claim that *Kofuku Maru* was the first Japanese ship captured by the RAN in the Pacific Zone, became fact. Both these claims have appeared in publications world-wide and were repeated on the television programme *This is Your Life*, which featured *Krait*, and on which some of *Goulburn*'s crewmembers who allegedly captured her appeared. Although the various sources disagreed on the date, it was widely accepted that this event occurred on either December 8, 11, 12 or 13, 1941 and that *Kofuku Maru* was towing either four or six barges at the time of her capture.

While it is indisputable that *Goulburn* captured a Japanese fishing vessel shortly after the outbreak of war, that ship was not *Kofuku Maru*. During the research for this book, the

Appendix I

Australian National Maritime Museum kindly made accessible to the author papers which had been confiscated from the Japanese ship which Goulburn's crew had captured. Because of the long accepted history that this captured vessel was Kofuku Maru, the Maritime Museum had no reason to doubt the authenticity of the papers, despite the fact that a name other than Kofuku Maru appeared on them. It has now been established that the difference in the names is not the result of a clerical or transcription error and that the papers belong to the ship so named — the vessel Shofuku Maru (Small Fortune).

It is not to be wondered that such an error of identity was made. With claims made by Goulburn's crew that she had captured Kofuku Maru accepted at face value and unchallenged for almost twenty years, fiction had inevitably become 'fact'.

The issue had become even more confused by the oft-repeated statement that Kofuku Maru was the first ship captured by the RAN in the Pacific Zone. Since the crewmembers of Goulburn's sister ship, HMAS Maryborough, knew without doubt that this honour belonged to them, Goulburn's claim had in recent years been hotly disputed. No one however, had managed to prove the claims either way.

After a lengthy investigation into the story, Major Hall and I have established that neither vessel has any claim to the capture of Kofuku Maru. However, we concede that such is the similarity of the names of the vessels involved that it is little wonder that confusion arose as people tried to remember what happened almost thirty years after the event.

On 8 December 1941, HMAS Maryborough, together with HM Australian Ships Goulburn, Burnie and Bendigo of the 21st Minesweeping Flotilla, additional corvettes and various other Allied vessels (including two Yangtse riverboats Grasshopper and Dragonfly and a Yangtse River gunboat, the 700 tonne Scorpion), was patrolling the waters off Singapore. All ships in this rather diverse fleet were under the control of Maryborough's Lieutenant-Commander Cant, RAN. At noon, when about forty kilometres from Singapore and only hours after war with Japan had been declared, Maryborough intercepted a vessel named Fukuyu Maru (Fortune of Excellence), registration number 2163. After shots were fired the vessel surrendered and a boarding party from

Maryborough took her over. *Fukuyu Maru* was then taken in tow to Singapore waters, where she was eventually impounded at the Naval Base. Three hours after the capture of this vessel, in keeping with the policy of checking on all shipping, enemy or otherwise, *Goulburn* stopped a launch towing a junk. After the vessels had hoved to, a party was sent in the ship's whaler to examine the other ships' credentials.

At 11.50 am on 11 December 1941, three days after Dickie Dickinson had impounded *Kofuku Maru* and all the other Japanese fishing vessels that were in port, and three days after *Fukuyu Maru* had been apprehended by *Maryborough*, HMAS *Goulburn*, which was patrolling with the rest of the flotilla about sixty-five kilometres from Singapore, was given orders to proceed to the Horsburgh Light where it was to take over a Japanese fishing vessel, the *Shofuku Maru*, and four barges (registered numbers 2205, 1597, 500, 133 and 284), which had been captured by US destroyer *Edsall*.

One minute after this signal had been received, *Burnie* signalled *Goulburn* that she had made contact with a submarine. At 12.10, ten minutes after placing a boarding party and prize crew on board the *Shofuku Maru*, *Goulburn* also detected a submarine, about 450 metres distant. Leaving Gunnery Officer N. O. 'Paddy' Vidgen, First Lieutenant Jack Langley, Petty Officer Sandy Boxsell, three armed sailors (Able Seamen Donald Johnston, Bertram Towner and the Engine Room Artificer) and the ship's multi-lingual Chinese steward on the Japanese vessel, *Goulburn* took up the chase for the submarine. After an hour's fruitless search by the two corvettes, during which four depth charges were dropped, *Goulburn* broke off the attack to retrieve Vidgen, Langley and the steward from *Shofuku Maru*. Boxsell and the three armed sailors were left on board to see that the enemy ship reached Singapore.

When Vidgen returned to *Goulburn* in the ship's whaler he brought with him two brass tubes containing *Shofuku Maru*'s confiscated ship's papers. Included among them were the identity papers of her captain Suburo Izimi and crewmember Eikichi Nagamine. To make matters even more confusing, Nagamine's papers showed he had been on another ship besides *Shofuku Maru* — the *Fukufu Maru* (Fortune of Wind). None of these papers

Appendix I

was surrendered to the RAN: Vidgen kept the identity papers, while *Goulburn*'s captain, Lieutenant-Commander B. Paul, RANR, retained the others. At 3.30 pm, with her crew once more on board and the whaler restowed, *Goulburn* rejoined *Burnie* to seek further submarine contacts for half an hour, when the search was called off.

Just on dusk at 6.40 the following evening, *Goulburn* was again ordered to proceed to the Horsburgh Light, this time to take over a Japanese fishing vessel towing six barges, recently captured by a British destroyer, HMS *Encounter*. By 8.15 a boarding party from *Goulburn* was lowered in the ship's whaler to relieve *Encounter*'s party, which then returned to the destroyer.

By the time Singapore fell on 15 February 1942, the tally of fishing vessels taken into custody was considerable. Indeed, for the month of December alone, there had been many small craft apprehended by Lieutenant-Commander Cant's flotilla, nineteen being captured on December 16 — fourteen by *Bendigo* and another five by *Dragonfly*.

It is therefore not surprising that, more than thirty years after the events of December 1941, incidents which occurred during the many patrols of HMAS *Goulburn* became telescoped and the identity of *Kofuku Maru* confused with that of *Shofuku Maru* and, occasionally, the other Japanese ship captured by *Encounter* on December 12. Moreover, it appears from the hand-lettered label on the brass cylinder which held the papers retained by *Goulburn*'s commander that Paul himself (despite the fact that the papers were clearly marked *Shofuku Maru*) believed them to be those of *Kofuku Maru*.

With Department of Naval Intelligence and other documents proving that *Kofuku Maru*, registered number 2283, was taken into custody in Singapore on December 8; *Maryborough*'s Letter of Proceedings and photographs taken at the time by one of her crewmembers proving beyond all doubt that the Japanese vessel captured by *Maryborough* on December 8 was *Fukuyu Maru*, registered number 2163; *Goulburn*'s log recording that *Shofuku Maru*, registered number 2205, was apprehended and taken as a prize on December 11; Vidgen's confirmation that papers were retained by him and Paul; and the internal configuration and paintwork of the ships being quite different (*Kofuku Maru* having her mast in the bow, four fish holds and white paint around the wheelhouse doors and windows; *Fukuyu Maru* having her mast stepped back and her wheelhouse painted a dark uniform shade; and the apparently twin-masted *Shofuku Maru* having one very large fish hold situated between the foremast and the wheelhouse), it is obvious that *Kofuku Maru*, *Fukuyu Maru* and *Shofuku Maru* are three quite distinct vessels. It is also obvious that the honour of capturing the first enemy ship in the Pacific Zone must belong to HMAS *Maryborough*.

It is highly unlikely that crew members of HMAS *Goulburn* would ever have had any cause to attempt to recall in detail the routine patrols of their ship had not *Krait* become a vessel of such significance — albeit long after the event. Indeed, information volunteered by Vidgen on the boarding of *Shofuku Maru* and the recollection of other crew members on the apprehension of the second ship on December 12 differ only in minor details from the entries in the *Goulburn*'s log. While it is understandable that the desire by *Goulburn*'s commander and crew to be associated with *Krait* has led to their offering in good faith information on the capture of a ship assumed by them to be *Kofuku Maru*, the unquestioned acceptance of this 'fact' is the reason why *Shofuku Maru* and, occasionally, the unnamed second vessel captured by *Encounter* and handed over to *Goulburn*, have assumed the identity of *Kofuku Maru*.

APPENDIX II

The tale of Sister Edith Stevenson: Survivor

The following story is taken from a first-hand, unpublished account, written by a missionary nursing sister, Edith Stevenson, after the war. Edith (then unmarried), who was working at the Queen Alexandra Hospital at the time, was ordered to leave Singapore on the evacuation ship SS *Kuala*, on Friday 13 February 1942. This edited extract, which takes up her story as she prepares to abandon ship near Pompong Island, gives not only a vivid account of her incredible will to survive, but of her outstanding courage in the face of appalling adversity.

'There were non swimmers holding on to bits of wreckage. I saw one woman grab a dead body only to let go when the truth dawned. Another lady, a nursing sister, who judging by her uniform was from the Government Hospital, was swimming very well and getting clear of the crowded area when a Japanese plane blew her to bits ... The top deck seemed a long way from the water. However there was no alternative. Time was short and the way to a lower deck was either blocked by dead bodies or frantic survivors. Blood from the casualties made the deck slippery. Without further hesitation, I left my small case of valuables on deck and slid overboard. It seemed better to die by drowning than be roasted alive. The heat from the fire on board was unbearable ...

'The sea water was nice and cool. I was trying to swim away from the sinking ship when a voice called out "Help me. I have two children in Australia. I must get to them." I was a bit hampered with clothing and was tired. I had had very little sleep for days and knew I could not support a grown woman.

'She clung to me like a limpet when suddenly a piece of wood floated by. I suggested we each held one end, leaving me free to swim and keep us both afloat.'

Shortly afterwards Edith was helped aboard a raft, but was asked to jump overboard to make room for another survivor.

'I jumped into the sea and swam alongside. Two other swimmers and myself tried, in vain, to tow the raft to nearby Pompong Island. What at first seemed very easy proved to be an impossible task. We had not reckoned with the tidal-races which abounded in the area. One minute we could almost touch the undergrowth around the island, the next, as if by magic, we were swept far out to sea. Each attempt became more exhausting. Eventually the gentleman swimmer said to the other nurse and myself, "Let us three make a dash to Pompong Island. I'm sure we could make it."

'Hearing this suggestion, a plea from those on the raft not to desert them ended in the other two swimming away. I stayed with the raft. I knew I could do very little, apart from keeping up morale. It seemed a terrible thing to desert them. I never met the swimmers again ...

'There were ten of us left on the raft. Nine on the raft and myself swimming with my uniform belt tied to the back of the raft. I was trying to tow it by swimming on my back. What I would achieve by doing this I did not know, but so long as we kept moving, there was hope. We were a mixed bag — two Indian Sepoys or Madrassi soldiers, a Sikh Havildar, two RAF corporals, an Anglo-

Appendix II

Indian lady, the Australian nurse [whom Edith had saved earlier], an old gentleman who had been the chief censor in Singapore and myself. We saw the *Kuala* nose-dive and disappear. Cries from survivors in the sea lingered for a while, but as we got further away, they ended.

'During the afternoon a Japanese plane flew overhead. We thought our time had come. Silently I prayed to God that after the ordeal we had come through, he would spare us further trouble. My prayers were answered. We saw the plane disappear and could scarcely believe it. Perhaps we were not seen, or maybe not worth a bomb. This gave us renewed strength of will to survive. Various distractions occupied our minds as we floated along. A strange fish jumped on to the raft — it was wedge-shaped and pink in colour. We kept it as possibly we would be hungry later on. On two occasions the old gentleman at the rear of the raft decided he was a nuisance and dropped into the sea. "He's in the water, miss", was the cry. I untied my belt, swam round and rescued him. In spite of his remonstrations that he was a hindrance and had "lived his life", I knew that if one person left, others would follow in despair. We got very thirsty as the sun beat down. The raft was just a few strips of wood nailed together. It had no provisions or water supply. With the sea all round us, there was the temptation to drink, but we knew the consequences of this. For some hours our spirits flagged. Suddenly there was a refreshing breeze. One of the RAF men took off his shirt, threaded it over a piece of wood and propped it up for a sail. It proved quite useless and was soon carried away. When it was beyond reach, the owner said there had been two hundred dollars in one of the pockets.

'When the reality of our situation became apparent, each of us got frustrated and cross. The Punjabis and Madrassi did not speak English and communications were difficult. They tried to help by paddling with their hands in the sea. I prayed throughout the day, vowing that if my life was spared, I would try to be a better person, never to let opportunities to help others pass me by.

'It was getting dark and must have been nearly 6 p.m. No one had a watch that was working, but in those tropical regions there is usually twelve hours of day, followed by twelve hours of night. The change from light to dark is very quick. There is no twilight. Once the sun goes down there is darkness.

'I felt very heavy and tired. My tissues must have been getting waterlogged. What could I do? To sleep in the water was out of the question. There was no space on the raft. Had I tried to get on it those already there would have prevented it. However useless this proved, it was taken for granted that I would stay where I was, towing the raft.

'Suddenly a tiny speck showed on the horizon. What could this be? My first thought was Japanese looking for survivors. We all yelled with what force our dry throats would permit. It was really too dark to see clearly. At first we thought the boat was going away from us, but in a short time it was alongside our raft. It was impossible to see what nationality these men were, and when they produced a knife I wondered were they going to kill me. In our nervous state we expected the worst. Soon they cut my twisted belt and pulled me into the boat. The others called "Leave her — she can swim." How they thought I could last any longer was beyond belief ...

'Another woman was also helped into the tiny boat. It was then full and the fishermen rowed away. They were Malays and hearing our cries for help had left their work to come to our aid. They rowed to a sandbank and returned to collect the others from the raft in relays. From the sandbank we were taken to a small island a short distance away. On the way they passed their hats round for any jewellery or money we had ... I had what remained of a gold expanding wristlet-watch, which had stopped at 9.30 a.m. It was now useless ... but the gold would be of value. I was only pleased to have something with which to show my gratitude.'

After being cared for by villagers for some time, Edith Stevenson and the rest of her party were passed on to Amir Silahili's rescue

Appendix II

organisation. After caring for the ill and wounded in every staging camp, she finally reached the mouth of the Indragiri River, where she joined the escape route to Padang. After a ten-day voyage Edith arrived safely in Ceylon, and went to India where she married a doctor, Captain Stevenson. She carried on with her nursing duties for the remainder of the war, then she returned home to the UK. It does not appear from the information available that she ever gained recognition for what must be regarded as an exceptional act of heroism.

APPENDIX III

Krait Crewlists

February–March 1942
William Roy Reynolds (Master)
Alec A. Elliott (Engineer)
Harold Papworth (Able Seaman)
Ah Tee and seven Chinese (deserted at Pulau Koendoer)
Looi Pek Sye (Stewardess/deputy helmsperson)
Ah Kwai (Motorman — deserted at Bengkalis)
Ah Chung (Motorman — deserted at Bengkalis)
Saitaan bin Abdulamid (Deckhand)
Frank McNeil (also listed as Frank McGrath, dismissed at Tambilahan)
and Looi Lam Kwai (aged three, daughter of Looi Pek Sye)

January 1943: Original twenty Jaywick team members
* William Roy Reynolds (Master)
  Captain Ivan Lyon (Commanding Officer and party leader)
  Lieutenant Donald M. N. Davidson (2IC)
* Captain F. G. Chester
* Sub-Lieutenant B. T. Overell (Explosives expert)
  Corporal R. Morris (Medical orderly)
* Leading Telegraphist D. Sharples
* Seaman A. Hobbs (Cook)
  Stoker Manson (Engineer, left the ship in Brisbane)

Appendix III

Leading Seaman K. P. Cain (joined the ship in Brisbane)
Leading Stoker J. P. McDowell (Engineer, joined the ship in Brisbane)

Operatives
Able Seaman A. W. Jones
Ordinary Seaman M. Berryman
Ordinary Seaman W. G. Falls
* Ordinary Seaman L. K. Hage
Ordinary Seaman A. W. G. Huston
* Ordinary Seaman S. F. McCabe
Ordinary Seaman F. W. Marsh
* Ordinary Seaman D. W. Russell
* Ordinary Seaman N. R. Wright
Note: Leading Seaman Johnson withdrew from the operation before *Krait* left Sydney.
* Denotes crewmembers who left the ship in Cairns.

September 1943: Final 14 Jaywick Team members
Those who remained from the original team were Major Ivan Lyon, Lieutenant Donald Davidson, Corporal Morris, Leading Seaman Cain, Able Seamen Berryman, Jones, Falls, Huston and Marsh, and Leading Stoker McDowell.

Newcomers were:
Lieutenant H. E. Carse (Navigator)
Lieutenant R. C. Page (Operative)
Leading Telegraphist H. S. Young
Corporal A. Crilley (Cook)

1944-45
Since the records are by no means complete, the following lists may contain omissions. Some dates of commencement may also be approximate.
Lieutenant W. K. Witt (Commanding Officer, February 1944)
Skipper T. N. Naylor (Commanding Officer, June 1944)
Sub-Lt. T. F. Wayland (Commanding Officer, October 1944)
Sub-Lt. Dann (Commanding Officer, December 1944)
Sub-Lt. H. Williams (Commanding Officer, February 1945)

ERA R. W. Mathers (February 1944)
ERA F. Brown-King (February 1944)
Sergeant Russel (February 1944)
Sergeant Hoffie (February 1944)
Lieutenant Key (June 1944)
Mate Davey (June 1944)
Seaman Harris (June 1944)
Seaman Hurren (June 1944)
Seaman Mather (June 1944)
Stoker Wilson (June 1944)
Stoker Aarons (June 1944)
Able Seaman Halgren (June 1944)
Able Seaman Turner (June 1944)
Seaman S. O'Dwyer (August 1944)
Leading Seaman Frecker
D. A. Campbell
Able Seaman Moore
Petty Officer Godfrey (February 1945)
Able Seaman Taylor (February 1945)
Able Seaman Tanner (February 1945)
Stoker Myringe (February 1945)
Sergeant Flinders (February 1945)
Lieutenant A. R. Chapman (1945)

References

Spelling
Because of great variation in the spelling of Indonesian and Malaysian place names, that which appears on the original documents, or, if inapplicable, on current British Naval Charts has been followed here.

Note: For more detailed references about information concerning the Fall of Singapore, Ivan Lyon, William Roy Reynolds, Operation Jaywick and The Double Tenth Massacre, see Lynette Ramsay Silver, *The Heroes of Rimau*, Sally Milner Publishing, Sydney 1990.

Books
Allen, Louis, *Singapore 1941–1942*, London 1977.
Australian War Memorial, *HMAS Mk IV*, Canberra 1945.
Baldwin, Suzy (ed), *Unsung Heroes and Heroines of Australia*, Melbourne 1988.
Barber, Noel, *Sinister Twilight*, London 1958.
Bennett, Lieut.-Gen. H. Gordon, *Why Singapore Fell*, Sydney 1944.
Bostock, J., *Australian Ships at War*, Sydney 1975.

Brooke, Geoffrey, *Alarm Starboard*, Cambridge 1982.
—— ., *Singapore's Dunkirk*, London 1989.
Caffrey, Kate, *Out in the Midday Sun*, London 1973.
Callahan, Raymond, *The Worst Disaster*, London 1977.
Churchill, Winston S., *The Second World War, Volume 2: The Onslaught of Japan*, London 1951.
Coates, Albert and Rosenthal, Newman, *The Albert Coates Story*, Melbourne 1977.
Cruikshank, Charles, *SOE in the Far East*, Oxford 1983.
Day, David, *The Great Betrayal*, Sydney 1988.
Falk, Stanley L., *Seventy Days to Singapore*, London 1975.
Fergusson, Bernard, *Wavell: Portrait of a Soldier*, London 1971.
Frost, Ted, *From Tree to Sea: The Building of a Wooden Drifter*, Levenham Suffolk, 1985.
Gibson, Walter, *The Boat*, London 1974.
Gill, G. Herman, *Australia in the War of 1939-45, Royal Australian Navy 1939-1942*, Canberra 1957.
Gilmour, Oswald W., *Singapore to Freedom*, London 1942.
Gough, Richard, *SOE Singapore 1941-42*, London 1985.
—— ., *The Escape from Singapore*, London 1987.
Great Britain Navy Department Navy List, 1918-1919.
Hall, Timothy, *The Fall of Singapore*, Sydney 1983.
Kirby, S. Woodburn, *Singapore: The Chain of Disaster*, London 1971.
—— ., *The War Against Japan*, London 1957.
Leasor, James, *Singapore*, London 1968.
Long, Gavin, *The Six Years War*, Canberra 1972.
McIntyre, W. David, *The Rise and Fall of the Singapore Naval Base*, London 1979.
Manual of Military Law, 1941.
Maxwell, Sir George, *The Civil Defence of Malaya*, London 1943.
Montgomery, Brian, *Shenton of Singapore*, London 1984.
Mooney, James L. (ed), *Dictionary of American Naval Fighting Ships, Vol VII*, Washington 1981.
Morrison, Ian, *Malayan Postscript*, London 1942.
Owen, Frank, *The Fall of Singapore*, London 1960.
Percival, Lt. Col. A. E., *The War in Malaya*, London 1949.
Poole, Richard, *Course for Disaster*, London 1987.
Rose, Angus, *Who Dies Fighting*, London 1944.

References

Silver, Lynette Ramsay, *The Heroes of Rimau*, Sydney 1990.
Simson, Ivan, *Singapore: Too Little Too Late*, London 1970.
Skidmore, Ian, *Escape from the Rising Sun*, London 1973.
Sleeman, Colin and Silkin, S. C., *The Trial of Sumida Haruzo and Twenty Others*, Edinburgh 1956.
Stevenson, William, *A Man Called Intrepid*, London 1976.
Smyth, Sir John, *Percival and the Tragedy of Singapore*, London 1971.
Swinson, Arthur, *Defeat in Malaya: the Fall of Singapore*, London 1970.
Stewart, Brigadier I., *History of the Second Argyll and Sutherland Highlanders*, London 1947.
Tsuji, Masanobu, *Singapore the Japanese Version*, Sydney 1960.
2/19 Association, *The Grim Glory of the 2/19 Battalion A.I.F.*, Sydney 1975.
Wigmore, Lionel, *Australia in the War of 1939-1945: The Japanese Thrust*, Canberra 1957.
Williamson, Kristin, *The Last Bastion*, Sydney 1984.
Wynyard, Noel, *Winning Hazard*, London c. 1948.

Despatches

Air Chief Marshal Sir Robert Brooke-Popham, Despatches to the British Chiefs of Staff, 28 May 1942 (*London Gazette*, Third Supplement, 26 February 1948).
Air Vice-Marshal Sir Paul Maltby, Despatches to the Secretary of State for Air, 26 July 1947 (*London Gazette*, Third Supplement, 26 February 1948).
Lieutenant-General A. E. Percival, Despatches to the Secretary of State for War, 25 April 1946 (*The London Gazette*, Second Supplement, 26 February 1948).

Documents
Australia
Australian Archives, ACT:
Papers Relating to Operation Jaywick and *Krait* (A3269 Item

Jaywick E2; AA 1978/155/1 Item 605/2D/1).
Correspondence, documents, minutes, reports, signals, summaries, etc. relating to Special Operations, AIB, SRD, LMS etc. (A3269/1 Items A24, D26, H1, H10, H14, H17, L1, L2, L5, L6, L7, O7, V5, V16, V17, W8, W9, Z1, Z2).
SRD History, Operations (A3270, Item SOA Vol 2 08).

Australian Archives, NSW:
Log of HMAS *Goulburn*, Navy Hydrographic Service, Log Books of HMC Colonial Ships, HMS and HMA Ships, 20-10-1855 to 31-12-1957 (SP 551 Bundle 238 3/12/41-5/3/42).

Australian Archives, Victoria:
Papers Relating to the Disappearance of W. R. Reynolds (Part of the Investigation into the Disappearance of Sachs and Perske), Department of Defence, Army Headquarters, Correspondence Files, multiple number series 1943-1951 (MP 742/1 File 336/1/1939 Pt 1).
Naval papers relating to HMAS *Krait*, Department of Navy, Classified general Correspondence Files 1923-50, (MP 1049/5 File 2026/27/296).
Report on SRD Operation 1, 29 June 1944 (MP 1587 File 114H).
Log of HMAS *Tiger Snake* (SP551-B578).

The Australian National Maritime Museum, Sydney:
Summary of material contained in Naval File 405/4/123, Wartime operations and Reports in relation to Operation Jaywick.
Papers of *Shofuku Maru*, captured 11 December 1941 by HMAS *Goulburn*.

Australian National War Memorial, Canberra:
AIB Activities 1942-1945, Press Release (AWM PR 85/325 Item 8).
Annual Reports of AWM, 1984-90, Statements of *Krait* Fund.
Doorpost from Balikpapan Borneo (AWM 20362, File 743/1/35, MM80).
Drawings and plans of HMAS *Krait*, September 1944, by crewman Sid O'Dwyer (AWM 3 DRL 7530).

References

Krait Memorial Dinner Souvenir (AWM PR 85/325 Item 8).
Krait Log (DRL 2515 File 419/17/3, Exhibition Document 154).
Log of *Krait*, March–April 1964; Voyage to Melbourne and Return (AWM PR85/20).
Papers of Albert Coates, including note from William Roy Reynolds, 24 February 1942.
Papers Concerning SRD matters etc., Papers of Field Marshal Sir Thomas Blamey (3DRL 6643, 45/56.3).
Letter of Proceedings, December 1941, HMAS *Maryborough* (AWM 78 [218/1]).
Oni 208-J Japanese Vessel Identification Manual.
Papers Relating to BBCAU (AWM 54 Item 376/5/29).
Papers Relating to Operation Scorpion (AWM 3/6643 Item 2/58).
Reports, Proceedings, HMAS *Krait*, March–August 1945; Reconnaissance Report to Aroe [Aru] and Banda Islands, 21 Oct 1945 (AWM 78 193/1).
Report on Activities of 2 Aust Contact and Inquiry Unit (AWM 52).
SRD Status Report, August 1945 (AWM 69 Item 23/57).
SRD Vessels, article by Peter Armstrong and Notes on Services Reconnaissance Detachment (AWM PR 85/325 Item 2).
Various Summaries of Proceedings of HMAS *Maryborough, Burnie, Goulburn*, 3 November 1941–7 March 1942 (AWM 69 Item 23/22).
War Diary of BBCAU HQ (AWM 52 Item 1/10/8).

Chief Secretary's Department, Sydney:
Papers and financial returns of *Krait* Appeal Fund (later named *Krait* Public Museum Fund) 1964-1990, Registered Charity Number CC 18692.

Naval Historical Records, Canberra:
Miscellaneous Notes on *Krait* (NHR File 52Y).
Summary of Proceedings of HMAS *Maryborough*, 3 November 1941–7 March 1942 (NHR 135e).

State Library of NSW, Mitchell Library:
Malayan Research Bureau Lists (ML 984/62).

United Kingdom
Guildhall Library, London:
Lloyd's Lists, 8 October 1923, 4 September 1924, 18 August 1943.
Merchant Navy List (M/F 18 568 Vol 12A and M/F 18 569 Vol 32).

Imperial War Museum, London:
Records of the Malayan Research Bureau, including Papers of Mrs G. Howell with correspondence from W. R. Reynolds, May–July 1943 and copies of Port Clearance Papers for *Suey Sin Fah*, March 1943; Details of Shipping ex Singapore; Excerpt from memoires of Mrs Edith Stevenson; An Account of the last voyage of HMS *Dragonfly*; Memoires of Marjorie de Malmanche.
Second World War Papers of Brigadier L.E.C. Davis.

Public Record Office, London:
Admiralty Files relating to Operation Jaywick (XC/3197 ADM 1/21966150; XC/B 3197 ADM 1/16678A).

United States of America
Department of Navy, Naval Historical Centre, Washington:
USS *Tuna*, 22 December 1943, Report of Landing of Allied Intelligence Personnel in Vicinity of Balik Island During Ninth War Patrol.

Minutes, Reports, Proceedings and Newsletters

ACT Advisory Council Minutes, Reports, Correspondence and Submissions regarding the purchase of *Krait*, 1961-63.
Broken Bay Newsletter, Vol 10, August 1991, article by Colin Simpson, RVCP.
Dedication Ceremony, *Krait*, 25 April 1964, Z Special Unit Association NSW.
Legal Papers relating to the ownership and the trusteeship of MV *Krait*, Royal Volunteer Coastal Patrol.

References

Minutes of the *Krait* Appeal Fund Committee and *Krait* Public Museum Fund Committee, 1962-1985.
Minutes and Reports of the Royal Volunteer Coastal Patrol *Krait* Division, 1977-78.
Minutes and Status Reports of *Krait* Public Museum Fundraising Committee, 1981-83.
Newsletter of Queensland Commando Association, October 1983.
Papers relating to the maintenance, care, control and usage of MV *Krait*, from 1963-1985, Royal Volunteer Coastal Patrol.

Newspapers/Periodicals etc
Adelaide Advertiser, 24 April 1981.
AIM, October 1973.
Air Sea Rescue Association of Queensland Journal, Vol. 2, No. 4, December 1982.
Australian Boating, July 1981.
Coffs Harbour News, 29 January 1982.
Australian Sea Heritage, Vols 3, 6, 7, 8, 14, 22.
Canberra Times, 22 June, 11 July 1963.
Central Coast Express, 28 February 1978.
Daily Mirror, 14 November 1978, 11 November 1981.
Daily Telegraph, 5 June 1982, 11 June 1983.
Forest Shire News, 31 January 1979.
Gold Coast Bulletin, 27 November 1982.
Illawarra Mercury, 4 and 29 August 1983.
Ports of NSW, June 1979.
Prologue, May/June 1982.
Saint George Leader, 15 July 1981.
Strike Swiftly (Journal of One Commando Association), September 1979.
Sunday Telegraph, 26 April 1964, 25 September 1983.
Sun Herald, 10 May 1981, 30 October 1983.
Sydney Daily Commercial News, 13 May 1981.
Telegraph (Brisbane), 6 March 1976.
The Age, 11 November 1974.
The Cairns Post, 12 August 1976.

The Courier-Mail, 15 April 1964, 6 October 1981, 2 and 12 April 1982.
The Daily Mercury (Mackay), 31 July 1976.
The Manly Daily, 5 July 1980, 12 September 1981, date unknown 1982, 22 January, 8, 15, 22 and 29 June, 7 July, 23 August, 15 October 1983.
The Melbourne Herald, 29 June 1963.
The Navy, October 1983.
The Northern Star, 22 April 1974, 5, 9, 11 February, 3 April, 17 September 1982, 11 June 1983.
The Sun (Sydney), 20, 21, 24, 26 and 28 June, 2, 3, 4, 5 and 8 July, 10 and 24 September 1963, 16 March, 28 and 29 April 1964, 31 May 1972, June and August 1972, January 1973, 3 September 1980, 23 April, 1 and 28 May, 14 July, 25 August 1981, 29 January, 19 February, 31 March 1982, 15 December 1983.
The Sun (Melbourne), 25 October 1974, 23 April 1981.
The Sunday Sun (Brisbane), 14 February 1982, 4 and 14 December 1983.
The Sydney Morning Herald, 6 March 1980, 20 October, 17 November 1981, 6 April 1983.
The Townsville Daily Bulletin, 7 August 1976.
Water News, October 1983.

Television Documentaries
Arms and the Dragon (BBC, London).
Patrol Boat (ABC, Australia).
Snakes and Tigers (Channel 10 Network, Australia).
This is Your Life, 25 April 1981 (Channel 7 Network, Australia).

Private Papers
Bert Bevan-Davies
Correspondence including letters from Paddy McDowell; L. Gardner and Sons, England and Hawker Siddley, Victoria. Various newspaper clippings on *Krait*, 1964-81.

References

William Cockbill
General Correspondence relating to MV *Krait*.
Records of Maintenance and Major work on *Krait*, 1964-84.
Photographic record of maintenance, usage etc 1977-82.

Tom Hall
Information, Correspondence, Photographs, Reports, Taped Interviews, copies of personal papers and documents, and written accounts from Abdul Rachman Achap; Admiralty, London; Australian National War Memorial; R. G. Barrett; Moss Berryman; Bert Bevan-Davies; British National Maritime Museum; Geoffrey Brooke; Cabinet Office, Historical Section, London; the late K. P. Cain; S. W. Carey; Rae Chambers; the Coates Family; Sylvia Crane; Alan Davidson; June Davidson; the Falls Family; Foreign and Commonwealth Office, London; L. Gardner and Sons Ltd, England; the late Dick Greenish; Hawker Siddley Pty Ltd, Sydney; H. M. Customs and Excise, Cardiff, Wales; the Huston Family; the Lyon Family; Colonel the Lord Langford; MacArthur Memorial Norfolk, Virginia, USA; the McDowell Family; the Marsh Family; Ministry of Defence, Naval Historical Branch, London; Francis Moir-Byres; Ron Morris; Roma Page; Port of Singapore Authority; M. Quinlivan; Registrar General of Shipping and Seamen, Cardiff, Wales; Margaret Reynolds; Royal Naval Historical Archives, London; Ruston Diesel Ltd, England; Horrie Young.

Lyon Family
Correspondence to the Lyon Family from various SRD and SOE personnel connected with Operation Jaywick.

Brenda Macduff
Diary of her wartime experiences (copy in Tom Hall Papers).

William Roy Reynolds
Logs of the *Suey Sin Fah*; Legal Papers; Marriage Certificate; Master's Certificate; MBE Citation; Naval Statement of Service; Newspaper clippings; Naval Commissions; Naval signals; Papers relating to *Krait*; Personal memos and notes; Photographs.

Lynette Silver

Information and Correspondence from Moss Berryman; Geoffrey Brooke; Les Clarke; Bill Cockbill; Deutz Australia Pty Ltd; the Fujisawa Family, Japan; L. Gardner and Sons Ltd, England; Senkichi Hamagami, Japan; Schichiro Kubo, Japan; Colonel the Lord Langford; Brenda Macduff; Marjorie de Malmanche; Ron Morris; Andy Munns; Nippon Kaiji Kyokai, Japan; Brian Ogle; Tony Onorato; RAN Archives; Bettina Reid; Ruston Diesel Ltd, England; Yoshio Shimizu, Japan; Colin Simpson; Tai-O Fishing Company, Japan; N. O. Vidgen; Yoshi Tosa.

Fred Spring

Design and technical drawings for proposed *Krait* Memorial Building, Australian War Memorial Canberra.

Index

Adamson, Lt 105
Agung, Mt 79
Ah Chung 38, 43
Ah Kwai 38, 43
Ah Tee 17, 35
AIB 52, 63, 100, 102, 115
Alatna HMAS 102, 103, 105, 106, 107, 108
Allah Muda Creek 43
Ambon 116, 117, 118
Amman, Pilot 41
Anaconda HMAS 114, 116
Anglo-Oriental Mining Co 2, 10
Argyll & Sutherland Highlanders 3, 5
Army Water Transport 138
Aru (Aroe) I 117
Ashmore Reef 108, 109
Australian National Maritime Museum 150-1
Australian War Memorial 133, 135, 146, 149

Bailey, Cmdr 6, 11
Bali I 79
Balikpapan 124
Ballarat HMAS 155
Banda I 117
Bangka Str 21
Barrett, R.G. 129-30, 135, 137, 144
Batam I 92
BBCAU 115, 116, 118, 119, 121

Began-Siapiapi 41, 43, 44
Bendigo HMAS 155
Bengkalis 41, 43
Bengku I 25, 27, 81
Bennett, Lt-Gen H. Gordon 51
Berhala Str 20, 23, 36, 37
Berryman, Mostyn 'Moss' 73, 74, 83, 84-5, 87, 93, 95, 97, 139
Bevan-Davies, Bert 65, 152
Bingham, Maj Seymour 107
Bintan I 20
Bisseker, F.D. 13
Blade, R.B. 128-9
Blakang Mati I 18, 19, 37
Blamey, Gen Sir Thomas 64, 120
Bombay 34, 47, 55
Bombay Sappers & Miners 2
Boxsell, Sandy 154
Branson, Cmdr 102
Brierley, Lt 106
Britannia 146
Brouwer Str 43
Browse I 103
Bukit Timah 12, 17, 21
Bulan Str 82, 89
Bullock, Capt 111
Burnie HMAS 155, 157
Burrell, Sir Henry 133

Cain, K.P. 'Cobber' 61, 71, 82, 102
Cairns 63, 65, 152

Campbell, Maj 'Jock' 33, 35, 46, 48, 52, 53, 54, 55, 56, 60, 69
Camp X 53, 56
Cant, Lt-Cmdr 155
Cardew, Dick 133
Carey, Capt Sam 66
Carse, Lt H.E. (Ted) 69, 71, 73, 74, 77, 79–85 passim, 92, 93, 94, 95, 100, 102, 119, 139
Chanticleer USS 75-6, 99
Chapman, Lt R. 117, 131
Chenko 24, 38
Chester, Capt 'Gort' 68
Christie, Admiral 99
Churchill, W.S. 10, 17, 21
Coates, Dr Albert (Bertie) 30-1, 35, 46
Cobra, Operation 107
Cockbill, Bill 141-50
Collins, Commodore/Vice-Admiral Sir John 51, 144
Colonial Office 64, 119
Country Craft 102, 105, 106, 107
Crane, Sylvia 138
Crilley, Andrew 70, 71, 80, 95, 100
Crocodile, Operation 115
Crowe, Dr Elsie 26

Danut 41
Davidson, Lt Donald 53, 54, 56, 62, 68, 71, 73, 75, 82, 89, 91, 92, 93, 94, 95, 99, 100, 101, 106
Diamond Snake HMAS 114
Dickinson, A.H. 'Dickie' 7, 13, 15, 17, 156
Dillon, Col 35, 47
Djambi R 37
Doddrill, WO W.F. 111-12
Dongas I 87, 89, 91
Double Tenth Massacre 97, 101
Dowling, Sister G. 29
Dragonfly HMS 19, 155
Durban HMS 18
Durian I 33, 81, 82
Durian Str 20, 33
Edsell USS 156

Eighth Australian Division 3
Elliott, Alec 18, 36, 44
Empire Star 18
Encounter HMS 157
escape route 24, 27, 31, 33, 81
Evans, Ray 113
Exmouth Gulf 73, 75, 76, 86, 96, 99

Falls, Wally 'Poppa' 71, 83, 91, 92, 95, 100, 106
Farrer, R.J. 3
FELO 52, 64, 115
Fergusson, Bernard 48
Ferrara SS 9
Firmament HMS 9, 14
Flinders Naval Depot 53
Force 136 India 121, 129
Frangestan SS 9
Fujisawa, Kotaro 16
Fukuyu Maru 16, 155-8

Galang I 82
Garden Island Naval Depot 53, 56
Gardner Diesel 64-5, 144, 152
Gardner, John 148, 149
Gnair 69
Goulburn HMAS 154-8
Gowrie, Lord 52
Grasshopper HMS 19, 155
Grass Snake HMAS 114
Greenish, Dick 131-5
Gympie HMAS 116, 117, 118

Hall, Maj Tom 133, 152-3, 155
Hardy, Drummer 5-6, 47
Hawkesbury R 53
Hazewinkel, H. 60
HDML 1324 113
Heather 103
Hobbs, Allan 'Bluey' 56, 68, 69
Huston, Andrew 'Happy' 71-2, 81, 83, 87, 91, 92, 100, 106

Indragiri R 23, 31, 32, 36, 45, 46, 163
Ipoh 2, 10, 37
Irish, Ray 148

Index

ISD 52, 64, 100

Jackson, Paddy 24
Japanese secret police
  (see Kempei Tai)
Jaywick, Operation
  awards for 100
  consequences of 97, 101
  early planning & training 51-6
  final plans 77
  initial concept 47-8, 49
  operation and raid 66-98, 151
  origin of name 49-50
  reaction by US 51

Jeffray, J.W. 111-12
Jensen, Harry 135
Jidda 9
Johnson, Maj T.C. 111-12
Jones, Arthur 'Joe' 73, 77, 82, 83, 87, 92, 95, 100, 139
Jupiter HMS 18

Kaag, Mr 37
Kampar R 48, 82
Karimoen I 36
Karinya HMAS 108
Keith, G.A. 19
Kempei Tai 97-8
Koendoer I 36
Kofuku Maru (see *Krait*)
Krait Bay 103
Krait
  as *Kofuku Maru* 13, 14
  capture of 17
  crewlists 164-5
  description of 15, 16, 17, 58
  Fund Committee 135, 141-50
  escape from Singapore 18, 19
  evolves into Country Craft 102
  immediate post-war activities 116-22
  in Darwin 99-114
  in Borneo 128-30
  in Sydney 1964-91 141-53
  Japanese origins 14, 16
  mistaken identity 154-8
  on Operation Jaywick 56-96
  problems in Australia 56-60, 62, 63
  problems in India 54-5
  rescue of civilians 20, 24, 29-31, 36-7
  return to Australia 131-9
  salvage claim 64, 119-22, 128-9
  voyage as a spy ship 35-6
  voyage as *Suey Sin Fah* 41-6
Kuala SS 25, 26, 41, 48, 81, 161
Kung Wo SS 25

Laburnum HMS 3, 5, 6, 13
Lagarto, Operation 107, 109, 110
Lingga I 31, 93
LMS 100, 101, 102, 105, 107, 115
Lombok Str 76, 77, 79, 82, 92, 94, 96
Long, Cmdr R. 52, 55
Looi Pek Sye 37
Lovelock, Bill 144
Lyon, Clive 68
Lyon, Gabrielle 68
Lyon HMAS 56
Lyon, Maj Ivan 32-3, 35, 46, 47, 51-6, 60, 64-5, 66, 68, 69, 71, 73, 74, 76, 77, 79, 83, 87, 89, 91, 92, 94, 96, 99, 100, 105, 106, 139, 153
Lyon, Dr Marjorie 26, 29, 47

MacArthur, Gen Douglas 51, 64
Macarthur-Onslow, Maj-Gen Denzil 135-6
McCaskie, Brig 121, 129
McDowell, Paddy 61-2, 66-8, 69, 70, 71, 75, 80, 87, 100, 102, 139
Macduff, Brenda 29, 152
MacKinnon, Sandy 142
McNeil (also listed as McGrath) Frank 38
Madras 45, 46, 47, 54
Malacca Str 33, 45
Malaya, invasion of 1-2
Malmanche de, Marjorie 26-7, 29, 152

179

Mandapam 55
Manderson, Mrs H. 77
Manson, Stoker 56, 60
Marsh, Frederick 'Boof' 71, 76, 83, 93, 97, 106, 138
Marsh, Mrs Ivy 138
Maryborough HMAS 155-8
Mason, Dick 144-5
Mecca 9, 48
Miller, R.W. 136
Moir-Byres, Francis 49-50
Morotai 116
Morris, Ron 'Taffy' 32-3, 35, 46, 48, 52, 53, 56, 58, 62, 69, 71, 73, 74, 76, 80, 99, 100
Mother Snake HMAS 114
Mott, Maj Edgerton 51-2, 64, 100
Mountbatten, Lord Louis 119, 132
M Special Unit 64
Mugger Project 103, 105, 108
Mulock, Capt 3, 6

Nagahama 14
Nagapattinam 45
Nankervis, A.R. 129
Navy League 149
Naylor, Skipper 105
Nellore SS 136-7
Newcastle 59
Nicobar I 45
Nobbs, Harold 136, 140, 141
Northam, Sir William 144
Nunn, Mr & Mrs Rex 21, 31, 47

O'Dwyer, Sid 111-12, 131
Ondina SS 75
One Commando Company 133, 135
Overell, Lt Bert 60, 68
Overell's Ltd 60, 77

Padang 33, 41, 46, 163
Page, Lt Robert 70, 71, 74, 79, 83, 87, 92, 99, 100, 106, 131
Page, Roma 131
Pandjang I 81, 82, 86, 89, 92
P&O Company 11, 55, 136

Papworth, Harold 18, 36
Parkes HMAS 113
Paul, Lt-Cmdr Basil 157
Pearlfisher 37
Pedang (see *Krait*)
Pelapis I 80
Penguin HMAS 148
Percival, Lt-Gen Arthur 3, 18, 20, 21
Peterson HMAS 59
Pittong I 84
Pompong I 24, 25, 26, 27, 29, 31, 80, 83, 92, 93, 94, 152, 160
Potshot Naval Base 75, 99
Prigi Radja 23, 30, 32, 33, 41
Pulau Kepal Kechil (Hill 120) 89, 91

Queensland Commando Association 146-7
Quinlivan, M. 131-2
Q ships 61, 102

Rabaul 66, 69
Rasak 43
Refuge Bay 53, 56, 58, 139
Rempang I 82
Rengat 23, 30, 31, 32, 35, 37, 44, 46, 47
Reymond, Lt Bruno 105, 106
Reynolds, Bridget (Bessie) 9, 127-8
Reynolds, Capt William Roy (Bill) 1-66, 68-9, 80, 119, 122-7, 136, 152, 153
Rimau, Operation 101, 105, 106, 107, 118, 133, 153
Rinjani Mt 79
Riouw Archipelago 20, 106
River Snake HMAS 105, 108, 109, 114
Rooseboom SS 47
Roti I 108

St John's I 18
Saitaan bin Abdulhamid 44
Sandakan 129, 137
Sandy I 103
Scorpion HMS 155

Index

Sea Snake HMAS 114
Seaton, Lt-Cmdr 55
Sederhana Djohanes 46-7
Semut, Operation 107, 115
Setstan SS 10
Sharples, Donald 56, 68
Shillong Shillong SS 55
shipping, Japanese attacks on 18, 25, 26, 27
Shofuku Maru 16, 156-7
SIA 52
Silahili, Amir 27, 162
Silver Gull 20, 24
Simson, Brig Ivan 4
Singapore, situation in 1-22
Singkep I 27, 31, 36, 28
SOA 64
SOE 52, 54
Soreh I 106
Special Operations 48, 101, 106, 115
SRD 64, 65, 69, 77, 96, 101, 102, 106-10 passim, 114, 115, 119-23 passim, 129, 150
Stevenson, Capt A.D. 110, 135
Stevenson, Edith 159-63
Stewart, Col 5
Stronghold HMS 18
Suey Sin Fah (see *Krait*)
Sugibawah I 31
Sui Kwong 30
Sungei Pakning 41
Sungei Siak 41, 43
Sunlag, Operation 110, 111, 112, 113
Supply 37, 56
Surabaya 76, 122, 125, 152
Sydney Maritime Musuem 150

Tambilahan 30, 41
Tandjung Bali 36
Tandjung Batu 36
Tandjung Pertandangan 45
Tandjung Pinang 20, 24, 27, 29, 36
Tandjung Pinang 25, 27
Tapai I 106
Telok Ayer 1, 3, 7, 17

Temiang Str 84, 93, 94
Thomas, Sir Shenton 45
Tien Kuang SS 25, 26, 27, 81
Tiger Snake HMAS 107, 108, 114
Timor 51, 109, 114
Tengorah 30, 37
Tortell I 84
Townsville 63, 66, 67, 70
Trappes-Lomax, Maj 52
21st Minesweeping Flotilla 155-8

United States' attitude to Operation Jaywick 51
United States Bureau of Economic Warfare 63

Van Brenkel, Controller 23
Vidgen, Lt N.O. 'Paddy' 113, 156-7
Vinette 49
Vischer, Controller 44
Voltaire, Cape 103
Volunteer Coastal Patrol 135, 140, 141-50

Walne, John 135
Warnaar, Controller 41-43
Warren, Col Alan 46
Wasp, Operation 103
Watts-Carter, Molly 27
Wavell, Gen Archibald 10, 11, 21, 48, 51, 52
Webster, A.G. & Sons 65
Wessel, Cape 73, 74
Williams, Lt Harry 110, 111, 112, 113, 117, 131
Willoughby, Gen 51
Witt, Lt 103, 107
Woodward, Sir Eric 139-40, 147

Yamashita, Gen 18
Young, Horrie 69, 76, 77, 80, 84, 96, 97, 139, 148, 149

Z Experimental Station 64, 68, 100
Z Special Unit 64, 150